Citizen's Basic Income

GW00673421

By the same author

101 Reasons for a Citizen's Income: Arguments for giving everyone some money

Bridgebuilders: Workplace Chaplaincy – a History

(ed.) *Diverse Gifts: Forms of Ministry in the Church of England*

Managing God's Business: Religious and Faith-based Organizations and their Management

Managing Religion: The Management of Christian Religious and Faith-based Organizations: Volume 1: Internal relationships; Volume 2: External relationships

Mediating Institutions: Creating relationships between religion and a secular urban world

Money for Everyone: Why we Need a Citizen's Income

(ed., with Jeffrey Heskins) *Ordained Local Ministry: A New Shape for the Church's Ministry*

(ed.) *Regeneration and Renewal: New and Changing Communities and the Church*

The Feasibility of Citizen's Income

(with Margaret Harris) *The Management of Religious and Faith-based Organisations: A guide to the literature*

(ed.) *The Parish: People, Place and Ministry: A Theological and Practical Exploration*

(ed.) *The Sermons of John Boys Smith: Theologian of Integrity*

(ed., with Sarah Thorley) *Together and Different: Christians Engaging with People of Other Faiths*

Citizen's Basic Income

A Christian Social Policy

Malcolm Torry

DARTON·LONGMAN + TODD

First published in 2016 by
Darton, Longman and Todd Ltd
1 Spencer Court
140 – 142 Wandsworth High Street
London SW18 4JJ

ISBN 978-0-232-53260-9

A catalogue record for this book is available from the British Library.

Phototypeset by Kerrypress Ltd, St Albans AL3 8JL
Printed and bound by Bell & Bain, Glasgow

Contents

Preface

This book has two purposes: to enable Christians to understand Citizen's Basic Income as a Christian social policy, and therefore one that Christians might choose to support; and to contribute Christian insights to the broad debate on Citizen's Basic Income. It is public theology, rooted both in the Bible and in mainstream social policy debate.[1]

So this book is not just for Christians interested in the ways in which tax and benefits systems affect our society: it is for anyone interested in the reform of tax and benefits systems and who wants to understand the contribution that the Christian tradition might be able to make to the debate.

First of all, the definition:

> A Citizen's Basic Income – often called a Basic Income, or a Citizen's Income – is an unconditional, nonwithdrawable income paid automatically to every individual as a right of citizenship.

The amount of the Citizen's Basic Income would vary with age (elderly people would receive more than working age adults, and children and young people less), but the amount would not vary in relation to any other conditions; it would be paid automatically, normally once a week or once a month; it would not be withdrawn as earnings, other income, or wealth, increased; it would be paid to each individual, rather than to couples or households; and it would be received by everyone legally resident.[2]

The nearest thing that we have to a Citizen's Basic Income in the UK is Child Benefit, which, apart from the fact that the main carer receives a different amount for the first child in the family than they receive for the other children, is an unconditional payment for every child, whatever the family's income, wealth, family structure, employment status, housing tenure, or anything else.[3] Every family receives the same amount for their first child, and every family receives the same amount for each of their second and subsequent children. Very similar to a Citizen's Basic Income is the National Health Service: free at the point of use for every legal resident, whatever their income or wealth. An unconditional income for every legal resident stands in the same tradition.

The idea of an unconditional payment for every citizen has been around at least since Thomas Paine in the eighteenth century: and ever since then the idea has occasionally re-emerged, only to fall back into obscurity. During a re-emergence thirty years ago a small group of us formed the Basic Income Research Group – now the Citizen's Income Trust – to pursue the debate through the seemingly inevitable trough in public interest. That trough has now ended with a bang, and almost every week we are seeing significant new expressions of interest among political parties, think tanks, the media, and the general public, much of it informed by the research undertaken and disseminated by the Citizen's Income Trust, by numerous similar organisations around the world, and by BIEN (originally the Basic Income European Network, and now the Basic Income Earth Network), which the Citizen's Income Trust helped to establish.

A substantial literature on Citizen's Basic Income now exists, including three books – *Money for Everyone*, *101 Reasons for a Citizen's Income*, and *The Feasibility of Citizen's Income* – by the current author: but when I searched for a book-length discussion of Citizen's Basic Income as a Christian social policy I could not find one. In 1988 Grove Books published my booklet, *Basic Income for All: A Christian social policy*, but that is now out of print; and in 1968 Philip Wogaman published *Guaranteed Annual Income: The moral issues*, but that was not specifically about Citizen's Basic Income, and that too is out of print. There are numerous published articles and unpublished papers on the relationship between the Christian Faith and Citizen's Basic Income, but there would appear to be no book on the relationship. This book is designed to fill that gap.

The book begins with a short introductory chapter that discusses the desirability and feasibility of a Citizen's Basic Income. Any reader who wishes to study the arguments for a Citizen's Basic Income in greater depth should read *Money for Everyone* or *101 Reasons for a Citizen's Income* (both published by the Policy Press); and anyone interested in questions of feasibility should read *The Feasibility of Citizen's Income* (Palgrave Macmillan).

Each subsequent chapter begins with a biblical text, outlines an aspect of the Christian Faith (no attempt is made to distinguish between doctrinal and ethical aspects), and then asks about the relationship between the aspect in question and the characteristics and effects of a Citizen's Basic Income.

The Citizen's Basic Income debate is global, so the book is designed for an international audience. Much of the material is presented therefore in entirely general terms, but in order to ground the discussion, I shall occasionally relate the more general discussion to the specific situation of the UK: to its society, its economy, and its tax and benefits system.

The book is designed to be used in two different ways. Either it can be read straight through, from beginning to end; or the reader can use the contents page to identify those particular aspects of the Christian faith and Citizen's Basic Income in which they are particularly interested. So that the book can be read in this second way, as far as possible, each chapter is self-contained, and in order to understand any particular chapter the reader should not need to refer to other chapters. Trying to ensure that each chapter is self-contained has meant a certain amount of repetition. I have tried to keep this to a minimum, and hope that the repetition that remains will not spoil the enjoyment of those who read the book straight through from beginning to end.

Whichever way you read the book, I hope that by the time you put it down I shall have persuaded you that Citizen's Basic Income is a Christian social policy. If I achieve that, then a corollary has to be that the Church – its members, its congregations, and its leadership – should join in the increasingly broad debate about Citizen's Basic Income, and should do all it can to see Citizen's Basic

Citizen's Basic Income

Income widely discussed. A specifically Christian contribution to the debate would not be new. In 1985 the Church of England report *Faith in the City* recommended that serious consideration should be given to Citizen's Basic Income as a solution to the problems of poverty and unemployment.[4] The Church – in the form of its congregations, as well as its denominational leaderships – might usefully reiterate this suggestion.

Malcolm Torry

Acknowledgements

There is a large number of people whom I must thank: my late uncle, Norman Usher, who as an assistant manager at Bexleyheath's Department of Health and Social Security office employed me during university holidays to file National Insurance stamp cards; the manager and staff of Brixton's Supplementary Benefit office, where I worked from 1976 to 1978 – and where I first understood the seriously inappropriate nature of means-tested benefits, and the considerable advantages of unconditional Child Benefit; Sir Geoffrey Utting, the Department of Health and Social Security's Permanent Secretary, for inviting me to the department's summer school when I was a curate at the Elephant and Castle in South London; and the staff of the summer school for introducing me to the briefly intense debate on Citizen's Basic Income that took place during the early 1980s.

I am particularly grateful for the invitation that I received to join a small group of researchers and other interested individuals who were meeting at the headquarters of the National Council for Voluntary Organisations – the group that then became the Basic Income Research Group, and subsequently the Citizen's Income Trust. It has been a pleasure to have been able to serve the Trust as its honorary Director for most of its existence; and I am most grateful to the Trust's trustees for granting me that privilege, and to successive Bishops of Woolwich for permission to spend time working for the Trust.

One of those bishops, Colin Buchanan, was responsible for establishing Grove Books in 1971, and in 1988 he republished as the Grove booklet *Basic Income for All: A Christian social policy* a booklet that my employer, the South London Industrial Mission, had previously published as *A Loaf of the Parish Bread*. I therefore owe to Colin a double debt of gratitude.

I also owe substantial debts of gratitude to the London School of Economics for encouraging my interest in unconditional benefits during the part-time M.Sc. course that I undertook there from 1994 to 1996, and for considerable generosity in granting subsequent visiting fellowships. Professor Hartley Dean of the LSE, and Professor Holly Sutherland and her staff at the Institute for Social and Economic Research at the University of Essex, have been most generous with their time as I have pursued my research into the desirability and feasibility of Citizen's Basic Income; my publishers, Policy Press and Palgrave Macmillan, have been most helpful; Karl Widerquist, editor of the series in which *The Feasibility of Citizen's Income* has been published, has been a constant source of enthusiasm and assistance; and it was Karl who introduced me to Philip Wogaman's *Guaranteed Annual Income* (1968), which otherwise I might not have found. To all of them I am most grateful.

The idea for this book germinated during a discussion between Barb Jacobson, Chair of Basic Income UK and a trustee of the Citizen's Income Trust, Becca Kirkpatrick, who was then working for Citizens UK, and myself, during which we recognised that it might be useful to create resources that might encourage Churches to take a major role in the Citizen's Income debate. I would also like to thank those members of the clergy of the Diocese of Southwark who participated in the afternoon session of the diocesan clergy study day in October 2015. A significant outcome of the day was the written reports on work that participants did together during that afternoon on connections between the Bible, themes associated with the Christian Faith, 'middle axioms' that might be suggested by those themes, and social policy. Many of the connections listed in those reports have found their way into this book. A similar event organised by workplace chaplains in Newcastle provided some additional connections.

I am most grateful to Greg Smith for reading an entire draft of the book and for making a large number of useful suggestions; and I am enormously grateful to David Moloney and his colleagues at Darton, Longman and Todd for their enthusiasm for this project, and for the work that they have put into it. (As always, of course, any remaining errors and infelicities remain the author's responsibility.)

As always, I owe a huge debt of gratitude to my wife Rebecca, for putting up with me spending days off and holidays over many years while I have tried to fit research and writing on Citizen's Basic Income around family life and my responsibilities as a full-time minister in the Church of England, and to agreeing to me retiring early two years ago so that I could continue with this and other research without burning out in the process.

And, as always, I owe a huge debt of gratitude to former and current trustees of the Citizen's Income Trust, and to all with whom I have worked so happily on Citizen's Basic Income during the past thirty years. I am grateful to the trustees for permission to use material previously published by the Trust.

All of the royalties earned by this book will be donated to the Citizen's Income Trust.

The views expressed in this book are those of the author, and are not necessarily those of the Citizen's Income Trust.

A note on sources

The main source is the Bible.

All biblical texts are taken from the *New Revised Standard Version* of the Bible, Anglicized Edition, copyright ©1989, 1995, the National Council of the Churches of Christ in the United States of America. Used by permission. All rights reserved.

Commentaries are only quoted where there is significant doubt as to a biblical passage's interpretation.

Secondary literature is only employed where it contributes to the argument.

Detailed arguments and references relating to many of the points made in this book can be found in my books *Money for Everyone: Why we need a Citizen's Income* (Policy Press, 2013), *101 Reasons for a Citizen's Income: Arguments for giving everyone some money* (Policy Press, 2015), and *The Feasibility of Citizen's Income* (Palgrave Macmillan, 2016). I have chosen not to clutter the text of this book with too many references. Any reader who wishes to follow up a particular argument will be able to do so by consulting the very full indexes of *Money for Everyone* and *The Feasibility of Citizen's Income*, and the contents page of *101 Reasons for a Citizen's Income*. I have only included in this book significant references that would not be found in any of those other three books.

A note on terminology

Alternative descriptions

A Citizen's Basic Income is an unconditional, nonwithdrawable income paid automatically to each individual. It has often been called a 'Basic Income': terminology that seems first to have entered the English language via the Dutch *Basisinkomen*, where *basis* means 'base' or 'foundational'. The problem with the English 'basic income' is that 'basic' in UK English (but not in American English) carries somewhat derogatory overtones. Something is 'basic' if it isn't the best.

For this reason, and in order to say something positive about an income for everyone, the Joseph Rowntree Charitable Trust asked what was then the Basic Income Research Group to refer to a Basic Income as a 'Citizen's Income', and to change its own name to the Citizen's Income Trust. The trustees agreed. While the word 'citizen' is not entirely unproblematic, at least 'Citizen's Income' does not carry the negative overtones of 'Basic Income'.

A Citizen's Basic Income has sometimes been referred to as a Basic Income Guarantee, or a Minimum Income Guarantee. Two words that we shall avoid in this book are 'guarantee' and 'minimum'. The problem with these two words is that they can apply to means-tested benefits, which are designed to ensure that a household reaches a 'guaranteed minimum income'. This idea could not be further from the idea of a Citizen's Basic Income. In the UK 'minimum' and 'guarantee' are particularly problematic because 'Minimum Income Guarantee' was once the name given to a means-tested benefit for pensioners.

Scotland's debate on the future of the benefits system is now diverging from the debate in the rest of the UK, and with the encouragement of the Citizen's Income Trust a group of Scottish researchers is now establishing a separate Scottish organisation to promote debate in Scotland. That group has decided to use the terminology 'Citizen's Basic Income': an option that has occasionally been discussed before. Independently, the publisher of this book, Darton, Longman and Todd, has suggested that I should use the same terminology in this book. I am happy to do so.

It is no problem that there is now a wide variety of terms for the same thing: Basic Income, Citizen's Income, Citizen's Basic Income, Universal Basic Income, Social Dividend … . All that matters is that they should all mean the same thing: an unconditional and nonwithdrawable income paid automatically to every individual as a right of citizenship.

A Citizen's Basic Income, Citizen's Basic Income, and Citizen's Basic Incomes

So far, we have used 'Citizen's Basic Income', 'Citizen's Basic Incomes', and 'a Citizen's Basic Income' interchangeably, and we shall continue to do so: although occasionally the context might demand one rather than the others. 'Citizen's Basic Income' always means the general idea itself: the proposal that every individual should be paid an unconditional and nonwithdrawable income. Where the reference is to a particular or generic individual's Citizen's Basic Income, an indefinite article or a possessive pronoun might be appropriate: 'a Citizen's Basic Income', 'their Citizen's Basic Income', and so on. 'Citizen's Basic Incomes' in the plural will generally refer to the Citizen's Basic Incomes payable to a particular group: 'Young people would receive smaller Citizen's Basic Incomes than older working age adults' – although 'a smaller Citizen's Basic Income' would also be appropriate here.

'A Citizen's Basic Income scheme' is a Citizen's Basic Income, along with the rates at which Citizen's Basic Incomes would be paid for each age group, and with a description of how the Citizen's Basic Incomes would be paid for.

Capitalisation

There is a convention that the proper names of UK benefits and taxes are capitalised, but general descriptions of taxes and benefits are not. So, for instance, 'income tax' means any country's tax on income, whereas 'Income Tax' means the UK's Income Tax

Marginal deduction rate

Someone on low pay and receiving means-tested in-work benefits, such as Working Tax Credits and Housing Benefit, might receive a pay rise. They might then be somewhat surprised that they were no better off. This is because Income Tax and National Insurance Contributions might have been deducted, and their Working Tax Credits and Housing Benefit will have gone down. The net result might be almost no change in their disposable income. The same can happen to someone unemployed who gets a job. They lose their Jobseeker's Allowance, they're paying Income Tax and National Insurance Contributions, and the net result is almost no change in their disposable income: and if they are now paying fares to get to and from work then they might be worse off than when they were unemployed.

Each of these individuals is suffering a high 'marginal deduction rate'. A marginal deduction rate is the total rate at which additional income taxes and the withdrawal of means-tested benefits reduces the amount that disposable income rises in relation to an increase in earned income. To take a particular example: An employee earns an additional £10. The additional earnings will be taxed, and if the employee is on means-tested benefits then those benefits will be reduced. Let us suppose that they find that their disposable income rises by £2. The marginal deduction rate will have been 80 per cent.

If a Citizen's Basic Income were to replace all or most of current means-tested benefits then the marginal deduction rates for many households would be lower. This would have a variety of different effects – which is why a Citizen's Basic Income's ability to reduce marginal deduction rates will appear in several of the chapters of this book.

Introduction

In this introduction I shall outline the different kinds of social security benefits (along with examples from the UK), offer a brief history of the UK's benefits system, show why change is required, describe the characteristics, desirabilities, and feasibilities, of a Citizen's Basic Income, and offer a brief history of the Citizen's Basic Income debate.

Benefits and tax systems

Most developed countries' benefits systems are composed of three types of social security benefit: means-tested benefits, social insurance benefits, and universal benefits. (A social security benefit that is unconditional will be universal, so an unconditional benefit will often be called a universal benefit.)

There are usually two types of means-tested benefit: 'out-of-work' benefits, given to adults of working age who are not in employment because they cannot find work, because they have onerous caring responsibilities, or because they are sick or disabled; and 'in-work' benefits, given to adults of working age who are in employment but whose wages are not sufficient to maintain a decent standard of living. Means-tested benefits are normally allocated to families or to households rather than to individuals. The amount of means-tested benefit that a family or household receives depends on the other income coming into the household and on the household's assets. (A means test is usually a combination of an income test and a savings test.) The higher the other income, the lower the benefit. Examples of out-of-work means-tested benefits in the UK are Income-based Jobseeker's Allowance (JSA) and Employment and Support Allowance (ESA), and UK examples of in-work means-tested benefits are Working Tax Credits and Child Tax Credits. Housing Benefit and Council

Tax Support (a rebate applied to a local property tax) can be paid both in-work and out-of-work. The new Universal Credit, which is slowly being implemented, is a combination of all of the main means-tested benefits.

Social insurance benefits are paid on the basis of contributions paid during employment or self-employment. The longer the contribution record, or the more money that has been paid into the fund, the higher the benefit. In some countries social insurance benefits are managed by the State, and in others by employers or trade unions. Benefits are paid out when a contingency occurs: for instance, unemployment or sickness. Benefits are generally time-limited, but not means-tested. Examples of social insurance benefits in the UK are the Basic State Pension and Contribution-based Jobseeker's Allowance. (If unemployment continues beyond six months then the means-tested Income-based Jobseeker's Allowance is paid instead.)

A universal or unconditional benefit is paid to people in a particular age group without means-test, and without contribution conditions having to be satisfied. An example in the UK is Child Benefit, already discussed in the preface.

Most tax systems are based on a progressive income tax. Each individual or household is allocated a tax allowance, and earnings up to the allowance are not taxed. Beyond the allowance, earned and other income is taxed, often with different rates applying at different income levels. In the UK, individuals rather than households are assessed for Income Tax.

Social insurance contributions will often be levied alongside income tax, by the State, by the employer, by a trade union, or by a regulated independent organisation. The UK's National Insurance Contributions are paid to the State alongside Income Tax. After an initial earnings threshold, contributions are collected at 12 per cent of earnings (but not on other income) up to an Upper Earnings Limit, and beyond that point they are collected at 2 per cent of earnings.

A brief history of the UK's benefits system[1]

From 1601 to the industrial revolution, the Poor Law required each parish to appoint overseers to spend locally collected tax revenue on relief for the poor on the basis of an assessment of means; and from 1834 a revised Poor Law consigned the poor to the workhouse. The Poor Law remained largely intact until the early twentieth century, when first of all an old age pension was established for the over 70s, and then contributory health care and unemployment insurance for selected trades. A patchwork of insurance schemes for illness, unemployment, and old age, continued to evolve throughout the first half of the twentieth century, with involvement from independent friendly societies as well as local and central government. A safety net subject to an often draconian means test remained in place. During the Second World War a committee chaired and managed by William Beveridge resulted in central government taking the reins in the form of a Family Allowance Act (to establish universal unconditional payments for the second and subsequent children in every family), a National Insurance Act (to establish contributory benefits for illness, unemployment, and pensions), a National Assistance Act (to establish a national means-tested safety net), and a National Health Service Act (to establish a health service free at the point of use).

The UK's benefits system has suffered from much uncoordinated tinkering since then, but it is still recognisably the system established by the 1942 Beveridge Report:[2] an unconditional Child Benefit (since 1979 for every child in the family), a contributory system for pensions and sickness and unemployment benefits, and a means-tested safety net (which serves far more households than Beveridge originally intended because means-tested benefits rates cover housing costs whereas contributory benefit rates have rarely been sufficient to do so.)

The history is one of progression from local to national and from simple to complicated. To quote from the 1942 Beveridge Report: provision of subsistence income was by a complex of disconnected administrative organs, proceeding on different principles, doing invaluable service but at a cost in money and trouble and anomalous treatment of identical problems for which there is no justification … a revolutionary moment in the world's history is a time for revolutions, not for patching.[3]

Beveridge could have written the same today.

The need for change

We are not at the moment in the midst of a world war, as Beveridge was, but we are at another 'revolutionary moment'.[4] Communication and information technology is dispensing with jobs of many different kinds; employment patterns are increasingly diverse and precarious; and family structures are increasingly diverse. Our benefits system, designed for a different era, is increasingly unable to cope. The UK's new Universal Credit (which is neither universal nor a credit) continues to assume both stable employment patterns and stable households, and is proving difficult to implement because that is no longer the world that we live in. A rapidly changing context requires an income maintenance system that does not need to adapt to changing circumstances – which means that the only candidate is the radically simple Citizen's Basic Income: the same amount, unconditionally, for every individual of the same age.

A particular problem imposed by means-tested benefits is that if the claimant gets a job, or if their earnings rise, then their benefits reduce in value. For too many households, the withdrawal of benefits, at the same time as Income Tax and National Insurance Contributions have to be paid, results in a total withdrawal rate of 96 per cent, so that for every extra £1 earned, the household's net income increases by just 4p. Universal Credit will reduce the withdrawal rate to 76 per cent, but that still provides little financial incentive.[5] The fact that fares to work can result in a negative overall financial outcome is one of the reasons for the increasingly onerous sanctions regime attached to Income-related Jobseeker's Allowance.Only a benefit that is never withdrawn as earnings rise can solve this problem.

A further problem is the increasing precariousness of employment. Someone unemployed might get a new job – but that job might last only two or three months, or perhaps only two or three weeks: or they might find themselves on a zero hour contract and that their working hours vary considerably from week to week. As they enter employment they might find themselves applying for Working Tax Credits and Child Tax Credits, and then, when they lose their job, closing that claim and claiming again for Jobseeker's Allowance: and then again putting in the vast amount of work required in order to obtain a new job – 'work for work'. The new Universal Credit will ease these problems to a small extent, but transfers into and out of employment, or between one employment and another, will still be administratively complex: and wages that change rapidly will cause even more problems. People who find themselves moving rapidly into and out of employment, or between short-term employments, or in employment with rapidly changing earned income, are in the 'precarity trap': an experience increasingly common for an increasing number of people.[6]

A problem that has always accompanied means-tested benefits is that only some members of society are subject to their conditions: so only some members of society face sanctions regimes, enquiries about intimate household arrangements, and penalties if small occasional earnings are not declared. Families not on means-tested benefits suffer from none of this. This is no way to achieve social cohesion. Only a benefit that is received by everyone, under the same conditions, can change this situation.

A Citizen's Basic Income's definition[7]

To reiterate the definition given in the preface: A Citizen's Basic Income – sometimes called a Basic Income, or a Citizen's Income – is an unconditional, automatic and nonwithdrawable payment to each individual as a right of citizenship.

- 'Unconditional': A Citizen's Basic Income would vary with age, but there would be no other conditions: so everyone of the same age would receive the same Citizen's Basic Income, whatever their gender, employment status, family structure, contribution to society, housing costs, income, wealth, or anything else.
- 'Automatic': Someone's Citizen's Basic Income would be paid weekly or monthly, automatically.
- 'Nonwithdrawable': Citizen's Basic Incomes would not be means-tested. If someone's earnings or wealth increased, then their Citizen's Basic Income would not change.
- 'Individual': Citizen's Basic Incomes would be paid on an individual basis, and not on the basis of a couple or household.
- 'As a right of citizenship': Everybody legally resident in the UK would receive a Citizen's Basic Income, subject to a minimum period of legal residency in the UK, and continuing residency for most of the year.

Citizen's Basic Income schemes

A 'Citizen's Basic Income scheme' specifies the levels at which Citizen's Basic Incomes would be paid for each age group, and the changes to the tax and benefits system that would be required to pay for the Citizen's Basic Incomes. A scheme would either phase out as many allowances against personal income tax, and as many existing state financed cash benefits, as possible, and replace them with a Citizen's Basic Income paid automatically to every man, woman and child, or it would reduce or remove personal tax allowances but would leave in place the current means-tested benefits system and recalculate each household's means-tested benefits to take into account the household's total Citizen's Basic Incomes. Either way, the scheme would:

- Create a secure financial platform on which all citizens would be free to build;
- Enable households to lift themselves out of poverty, because for anyone currently on means-tested benefits – whether out-of-work benefits or in-work 'tax credits' – marginal deduction rates would be lower than they are now, so additional earned income would result in more additional net income;
- Boost employment incentives: another effect of the reduction in marginal deduction rates for people currently on means-tested benefits;
- Bring about social cohesion. Everybody would be entitled to a Citizen's Basic Income and everybody would pay tax on all or most other income;
- Be affordable within current revenue and expenditure constraints;
- Be easy to understand. It would be a universal entitlement based on citizenship that is non-contributory, non-means-tested, and non-taxable;
- Be cheap to administer and easy to automate;
- End perverse incentives that discourage savings (savings reduce means-tested state pensions, so means-tested pensions discourage saving for retirement).

Payments would be automatic. Each week, or each month, every legal resident would automatically be given the Citizen's Basic Income appropriate to his or her age. For most adults this could be done through the banking system, and for children it could be done through the bank accounts of their parents. For those few adults without bank accounts special provisions would be necessary. Larger Citizen's Basic Incomes might be paid to older people, and smaller Citizen's Basic Incomes to children and young people, but there would be no differences on account of gender or marital status, nor on account of work status, contribution record, or living arrangements.

The Citizen's Basic Incomes would be tax-exempt and without a means test, but tax would be payable on all other income. The rate of tax would depend on the Citizen's Basic Income amounts. The higher the Citizen's Basic Income, the higher the Income Tax rate.

There are various ways of funding a Citizen's Basic Income. The particular schemes discussed in the appendix are funded by removing some tax allowances, increasing slightly the rate at which Income Tax is paid, and reducing or abolishing some means-tested and contributory benefits. But a Citizen's Basic Income could also be part of a wider tax reform package including, for example, mechanisms to tax company profits in the country in which the profits are generated, a land value tax, a financial transaction tax, or a carbon tax.

At the point of implementation, either means-tested benefits could be abolished, or some or all of them could be retained and everybody's in-work and out-of-work means-tested benefits recalculated to take into account their Citizen's Basic Incomes. A Citizen's Basic Income could either be implemented for everybody at the same time, or successively for different age groups.

Citizen's Basic Income's distinctive characteristics

There would be six fundamental differences from current means-tested benefits:

- *Citizenship would become the basis of entitlement*, subject to a minimum period of legal residency in the UK, and continuing residence in the UK for most of the year. Every citizen would have a small independent income, whether or not they were in paid employment.
- *The individual would be the tax/benefits unit.* The Citizen's Basic Income would be paid on the basis of the individual, and not on the basis of a couple, a family, or a household. Unlike the existing benefits system, Citizen's Basic Income would be symmetrical between men and

women. Marriage, civil partnership and cohabitation would be neither subsidised nor penalised.

- *The Citizen's Basic Income would not be withdrawn as earnings and other income rises*, nor would it be reduced by owning assets. It would be a base on which to build without having to report to officials every minor change in earnings or household composition. Benefits errors and fraud would be reduced significantly. Work and savings of all types would be encouraged.

- *There would be no availability-for-work rule.* Under the current system, young people in education or training, and unemployed people who study or train for more than a few hours a week, forfeit most benefits. This would not happen to their Citizen's Basic Income. School attendance, caring for children or other relatives, further and higher education, voluntary work, vocational training and re-training, would not be discouraged or penalised by the tax and benefits system in the way that they are now.

- *Access to a Citizen's Basic Income would be easy and unconditional.* Instead of the current maze of regulations, often resulting in perverse incentives, everybody would know their entitlement. Take-up would be nearly 100 per cent, as it is with Child Benefit (currently the only benefit close to a Citizen's Basic Income in the UK).

- *Benefit levels would be indexed to average earnings, or to incomes, or to GDP per capita, rather than to prices.* To index the Citizen's Basic Income lower than this would merely store up problems for the future. While all citizens would benefit from a more generous payment, there would be an equal and opposite pressure against Income Tax rises to fund it.

Questions

To suggest that the State should simply give everyone some money raises some fairly obvious questions:

Would people still work?

Under the current system, in spite of sizeable benefit withdrawal rates (or 'marginal deduction rates', MDRs), the vast majority of working age adults choose to seek employment. With a Citizen's Basic Income most people's marginal deduction rates would fall,[8] making it even more likely that working age adults would seek employment.

At the moment, parents and other carers can find that employment for a few hours a week brings only small financial gains – again, because of high marginal deduction rates. A Citizen's Basic Income would reduce this problem, so that working age carers who cannot or do not wish to seek full-time employment would be more likely to seek part-time employment. With today's benefits system, a flexible employment market can be a problem. A benefits system based on a Citizen's Basic Income would make a more flexible employment market more possible and more productive for both employers and employees.

Is it fair to ask people in employment to pay for everyone to receive a Citizen's Basic Income?

As a society we have chosen to fund payments to those not in paid work out of general taxation: so at the moment those in employment pay for benefits for people who are not. With Citizen's Basic Income both those currently receiving means-tested benefits and tax credits and those not currently receiving them would receive a Citizen's Basic Income. This would be a lot fairer.

Isn't guaranteeing a right to work a better way to prevent poverty?

The best way to prevent poverty is through well-paid employment; and the best way to ensure employment's widespread availability is to reduce the rigidities in the labour market that serve neither employers nor employees. A Citizen's Basic Income would help to achieve this. A Citizen's Basic Income in combination with a National Minimum Wage or a Living Wage would go a long way towards preventing poverty.[9]

Why pay money to the rich when they don't need it?

Simply because it is more efficient to pay the same amount to everyone than to run complicated means-testing systems. And in any case, because their Personal Income Tax Allowances would have been removed, the rich would be paying more Income Tax, so they would be no better off than they are now.

What about the particular needs of elderly people and people with disabilities? And what about housing costs?

Some groups of people need more money than others: particularly the elderly, because they are less able obtain employment income, and they might not have sufficient occupational or private pensions; and people with disabilities, both because they might have expensive care needs and because they might be less able to obtain employment income than other working age adults. Most Citizen's Basic Income schemes assume Citizen's Basic Incomes at higher levels for elderly people (often termed Citizen's Pensions); and most Citizen's Basic Income schemes retain separately regulated and administered benefits specifically for people with disabilities – separately regulated and administered because by definition a Citizen's Basic Income is unconditional and so has to be paid at the same rate for everyone of the same age.[10]

If there were no specifically Christian case for Citizen's Basic Income, the advantages that it would offer would be a perfectly adequate argument for implementing it.

A detailed case study of two possible Citizen's Basic Income schemes for the UK can be found in the appendix at the end of the book.

A brief history of the Citizen's Basic Income debate[11]

At the end of the eighteenth century, Thomas Paine wrote that because the planet is the common property of the human race, those who have taken control of the land owe a regular income to 'every person, rich or poor … because it is in lieu of the natural inheritance, which, as a right, belongs to every man … .'[12]

Ever since then the idea has found advocates. Following Mabel and Dennis Milner's and Bertram Pickard's foundation of the State Bonus League during the early years of the twentieth century, the most concerted attempt to promote debate on Citizen's Basic Income was Juliet Rhys Williams' minority report in opposition to the Beveridge Report in 1942. Her son, Brandon Rhys Williams MP, followed in his mother's footsteps by proposing a Citizen's Basic Income to a parliamentary select committee in 1982. Between the two Rhys Williams' interventions, in 1966 a briefly vigorous debate took place in the United States, and the idea was given an airing in a variety of countries. But there was no institutional focus for the discussions, so they quickly petered out: and it was to solve this problem that in 1984 the Basic Income Research Group – now the Citizen's Income Trust – began its research and educational activity. During the past thirty years the debate has become global, with numerous national and international networks involved, and increasing numbers of national governments, political parties, academics, think tanks, and journalists contributing to the debate, and to the growing number of pilot projects.

A Christian contribution to the debate[13]

It has been a pleasure to see significant recent interest in the relationship between Christian theology and the economy.[14] What is now required is a debate on the relationship between Christian theology and the tax and benefits system, for this particular aspect of social policy is one to which Christians can bring a distinctive viewpoint.

This book is specifically a Christian contribution to the debate. For the last half of my time as a full-time minister of the Church of England I worked closely with members of other faiths, particularly in the context of the multi faith Greenwich Peninsula Chaplaincy. It was a pleasure to do so. Among many other things, I learnt that other faiths have significant contributions to make to debate on social policy: and I also learnt that only members of a faith community can legitimately and effectively speak for it. In this book I shall not attempt to speak for other faiths: but I hope that its Christian contribution will be an encouragement to members of other faiths to make their own contributions to the debate on Citizen's Basic Income.

The heart of the Christian Faith is the conviction that God has lived a human life in the person of Jesus of Nazareth. Jesus lived and proclaimed the Kingdom of God, of which his resurrection is a firm promise. During the two thousand year history of the Church, Christians have explored many aspects of their faith, and have developed insights based on their experience and on the experience of the earliest Christians. Many of those insights are expressed in the New Testament, and some have developed since then. Many of them will be useful to us as we shape our contribution to the Citizen's Basic Income debate. The Kingdom of God has so far been lived in its fullness by only one man: Jesus of Nazareth; and its complete fulfilment is still in the future: but in our own time we can and should seek to shape our own societies in accordance with our understanding of the characteristics of the Kingdom of God, so that our societies can become expressions of hope for the Kingdom's coming. The many aspects of the Christian Faith that we shall explore in this book will inform our work in the tax and benefits field in the hope that our societies' tax and benefits systems might more closely mirror the character of the Kingdom of God and be a signpost towards the Kingdom's coming.

An exploration of the relationship between the Christian Faith and social and economic policy is best conducted by enabling the Christian scriptures and the broader social and economic policy debate to hold a dialogue with each other.[15] The rest of this book will therefore consist of short chapters, each of which will begin with what I take to be a relevant quotation from the Bible. In the New Testament we find the earliest Christian reflection on the Christian Faith, and therefore the insights closest in time to the influence of Jesus himself; and in the Hebrew Scriptures – the Christian Old Testament – we find literature that inspired Jesus' life and teachings, and so some of the biblical material will be taken from the Old Testament. The biblical text will be followed by a brief exposition of the aspect of the Christian Faith concerned, or of the insight that Christians have developed, and then by further texts and discussion: and then we shall ask how the aspect or insight on which the chapter is reflecting might inform our contribution to the Citizen's Basic Income debate.

In some cases we might move straight from the exposition of an aspect of the Christian Faith to a discussion of a Citizen's Basic Income scheme, but in other cases we might insert an additional stage: a 'middle axiom' (or, as William Temple put it, we might move from 'primary Christian principles' to 'derivative Christian principles', and from there to specific policy proposals[16]).

Middle axioms are

> maxims for conduct which mediate between fundamental principles and the tangle of particular problems.[17]

To take an example: the argument might move straight from a discussion of the grace of God – God's unconditional love – to a connection with unconditional benefits; or we might argue from grace to generosity, and then from generosity to unconditional benefits.

In the context of this book, no distinction will be made between Christian doctrine – the progressive systematising of the Christian Faith – and Christian ethics – a systematising of behavioural norms.

Such a distinction might be appropriate in the context of the individual, but it will rarely be appropriate in relation to social institutions such as money, taxation, and social security benefits. Here the Church and individual Christians have a responsibility to contribute whatever we can to widespread debate. Some of what we contribute might be better termed 'doctrinal' – such as the centrality of grace to our understanding of God; and some might be better termed 'ethical' – such as the dignity of the individual person,[18] and the importance of relationships and of community: but relationships and community have as much connection with God's nature as Trinity – as Father, Son, and Holy Spirit – as they do with any 'ethical' teachings relating to them in the New Testament and the Church's tradition; and unconditional generosity has as much to do with Christian ethics as it has to do with Christian doctrine. Paul's call to the Churches of his time to reflect in their own actions the generosity of God was both a doctrinal and an ethical appeal.[19]

Since biblical times there has of course been a wealth of reflection on the relationship between social policy and Christian doctrine and ethics. Each branch of the Christian Church – Orthodox, Catholic, Reformed, Anglican, Free Church, Evangelical, Pentecostal – has its own contribution to offer. In a short book of this nature it would be impossible to summarise the particular insights that each branch might wish to contribute. I hope that the biblically-based treatment that I have provided will encourage further contributions from within Catholic social thought, the Anglican social tradition, Wesleyan economics, and so on.

So from two thousand years of reflection on Christian belief and practice – including reflection on the Hebrew Scriptures – we shall choose a variety of aspects of the Faith and a variety of Christian insights; we shall make connections with tax and benefits policy; and in particular we shall employ aspects of the Christian Faith and Christian insights to evaluate Citizen's Basic Income as a reform option.

Citizen's Basic Income would celebrate God-given abundance

The earth is the Lord's and all that is in it,
the world, and those who live in it;
for he has founded it on the seas,
and established it on the rivers.

(Psalm 24:1–2)

The first creation narrative in the Book of Genesis[1] lists the stages of creation in a remarkably accurate order, and after each stage it says: 'God saw that it was good'. After God had put the final touches to it all by creating human beings, 'God saw everything that he had made, and indeed, it was very good.' The second and rather different creation narrative is equally convinced of the goodness and abundance of God's creation:

> Out of the ground the Lord God made to grow every tree that is pleasant to the sight and good for food, the tree of life also in the midst of the garden, and the tree of the knowledge of good and evil. A river flows out of Eden to water the garden, and from there it divides and becomes four branches. The name of the first is Pishon; it is the one that flows around

the whole land of Havilah, where there is gold; and the gold of that land is good; bdellium and onyx stone are there.[2]

The Psalms celebrate not only the goodness and abundance of the created order, but God's continuing care for it:

> You visit the earth and water it,
> you greatly enrich it;
> the river of God is full of water;
> you provide the people with grain,
> for so you have prepared it.
> You water its furrows abundantly,
> settling its ridges,
> softening it with showers,
> and blessing its growth.
> You crown the year with your bounty;
> your wagon tracks overflow with richness.
> The pastures of the wilderness overflow,
> the hills gird themselves with joy,
> the meadows clothe themselves with flocks,
> the valleys deck themselves with grain,
> they shout and sing together for joy.[3]

The creation narratives and the Psalms constituted an important part of Jesus' religious heritage, and so, not surprisingly, we find him combining celebration of God-given abundance and God's continuing care for us:

> Look at the birds of the air; they neither sow nor reap nor gather into barns, and yet your heavenly Father feeds them. Are you not of more value than they? … And why do you worry about clothing? Consider the lilies of the field, how they grow; they neither toil nor spin, yet I tell you, even Solomon in all his glory was not clothed like one of these. But if God so clothes the grass of the field, which is alive

today and tomorrow is thrown into the oven, will he not much more clothe you … ?[4]

Is there anyone among you who, if your child asks for bread, will give a stone? Or if the child asks for a fish, will give a snake? If you then, who are evil, know how to give good gifts to your children, how much more will your Father in heaven give good things to those who ask him![5]

In this age both of austerity and of increasing understanding that the world's resources are finite, we can easily forget just how abundant those resources are. The energy that the Earth receives from the sun is more than enough to provide for our needs if only we were sensible enough to provide the infrastructure required for capturing it. The world can produce more than enough food for everyone if we don't waste it, if we distribute it more equitably, and if we eat less meat. There would be no shortage of housing if more people lived together. There would be no water shortage if we were to reduce carbon emissions and arrest climate change. It might be true that 'enough is enough',[6] but it is equally true that there is enough for everyone. And not only is there enough for everyone: it is simply given. It is not we who create it in response to our needs.[7] By our labour we might co-operate with God in creation, but the abundance is God's gift to us. The air, the water, the soil, the energy … it is all an abundant gift. We therefore have no right to deprive anybody of any of it. God has created a world – 'the Earth is the Lord's'[8] – and has given it to all of us to share. This was the point that Thomas Paine made in the eighteenth century,[9] and that William Temple, Archbishop of Canterbury from 1942 to 1944, made in terms of St Ambrose's argument that

nature produced all things for the common use of all … and … nature produced the common right of property, but usurpation the private right.[10]

Wealth is God's gift, and it is intended for the common good, and not for accumulation by a few to the exclusion of the many:[11] so if we find that the gift has not been shared out as originally intended, then surely it is our responsibility to ensure that it should be, which means collecting resources from those who have benefited disproportionally from their position in the economy in order to pay to every individual a share of the wealth that properly belongs to everyone. A similar secular argument can be made. The physical and social capital from which we all now benefit has been built up by many generations of hard work, and it belongs to all of us, not just to a few. It is therefore right to collect some of the proceeds of that shared capital from those who have ended up with a disproportionate share, so that we can pay to every member of society a share of the wealth that properly belongs to everyone.

I am not suggesting for one minute that private property rights ought to be abrogated, or that individuals ought not to seek to own property, or that it is wrong to acquire a freehold on land. Private property rights have proved their economic and social value. The only thing wrong with private property is that it does not recognise the fact that land and every other natural resource is an equal gift to all of us. The economic deficit that so many people suffer can easily be ameliorated by distributing in equal proportions to every member of the community some of the proceeds that accrue to property ownership. The logic suggests that the distribution should be global,[12] but in the short to medium term that is likely to be impractical. A good second best would be a national distribution of a proportion of the proceeds from property ownership.

For the Christian, both the religious and the secular arguments are relevant. We have received generous gifts from God and from our forebears, and to all of them we owe gratitude. No gratitude is due to property owners.[13] Gratitude is due to God, to the many generations who have gone before us, and to all those who work hard to realise the potential of God's abundant gifts. A Citizen's Basic Income, paid regularly to every member of society, would be simply a just distribution of the proceeds of a common inheritance. How those resources should be collected in order to be distributed is of course an important question, which we shall tackle in a later chapter of this book, although here it might usefully be said that a land value tax might be a method more appropriate to the situation than a tax on earned income. But the major point is that the act of generosity is not that of any individual or group: the generous activity is God's, or it is that of the builders and inventors of the past. Jesus asks us not to be anxious about having enough to eat and enough to wear.[14] For many families, such anxiety is a constant and understandable fact of life; and, for too many, occasional visits to foodbanks are a necessity. By giving to everybody a share of God's abundance we would materially reduce the anxiety that so many families experience, we could put foodbanks out of business,[15] and the permanent financial security that Citizen's Basic Incomes would provide would for the first time enable us to experience what Jesus was wanting us to experience: a life without financial anxiety. That wasn't all that he meant by a life that was 'abundant',[16] or one characterised by 'complete joy',[17] but it would shift all of us a lot further in that direction.

The first book of Chronicles records David collecting together everything that his son Solomon would require to build a temple, and it records his prayer:

> But who am I, and what is my people, that we should be able to make this freewill-offering? For all things come from you, and of your own have we given you. … O Lord our God, all this abundance that we have provided for building you a house for your holy name comes from your hand and is all your own.[18]

2.

Citizen's Basic Income would be an act of grace

And the Word became flesh and lived among us, and we have seen his glory, the glory as of a father's only son, full of grace and truth. … From his fullness we have all received, grace upon grace.

(John 1:14–16)

At the heart of the Christian Faith is the grace of God: a nonwithdrawable love, an unconditional generosity. We do not earn God's love: it is simply a gift. God's primary act of grace is the giving of himself,[1] whether expressed as the sending of the Word, as the sending of the Son, or as God living a human life and experiencing the suffering that that entailed: but grace also characterises every relationship between God and the created order, God and the human race, God and each individual. Grace describes the very nature of God, and not simply something that God might choose to do.[2]

For a Christian, the primary reason for pursuing the Citizen's Basic Income debate has to be that a Citizen's Basic Income reflects the heart of the Christian faith. The unconditionality at the heart of the Christian Gospel finds an echo in the unconditionality at the heart of Citizen's Basic Income. In the UK, Child Benefit, free travel for elderly people, the Winter Fuel Allowance, free education for every child, and the National Health Service, already represent the grace of God in the social policy field. To establish a Citizen's

Basic Income would turn our social security system into even more of a signpost towards a Kingdom of God characterised by grace: that is, by unconditional generosity.

Here a certain amount of clarification is in order. The generosity that we are discussing here is not the generosity of one individual to another, nor of one section of a population to another section, as occurs when taxpayers are paying tax and unemployed people are receiving means-tested benefits. Neither is it 'charity', which divides us into donors and recipients, and keeps the donors in control. The Christian argument is that a Citizen's Basic Income represents *God's* generosity, and that nobody is left out of that generous activity:

For the grace of God has appeared, bringing salvation to all:[3]

– not grace just for an individual, nor grace for each individual one after the other, but what Tony Walter calls 'public grace'.[4]

But that is not the end of the story, because a gift can inspire a gift in response. Thus Jesus' words in Matthew's gospel offer an invitation:

You received without payment; give without payment.[5]

As Ronald Preston has put it: 'The radical offer precedes the radical demand'.[6] We have freely received, and so are invited to freely give. Paul makes the same point when he writes of the Church in Macedonia that the grace of God that they had experienced was the root of their financial generosity to the Church in Judaea.[7]

A Citizen's Basic Income would have the same effect. Freely to receive from society as a whole an unconditional and nonwithdrawable income would be an invitation to contribute to society – not only because for many households additional earnings would translate into more additional net income than they do now, and so would give them more to give to others, but also because to receive a gift is to invite a response: in caring work in the family and among neighbours, and in voluntary activity in the community.

We used to live in Greenwich, and every year, one Sunday in late April, we would have to plan carefully if we wanted to go anywhere. We were surrounded by the route of the London Marathon, and from early morning until mid-afternoon nobody could cross the roads. The entirely charitable London Marathon generated massive amounts of voluntary support. Volunteers worked from early morning until the afternoon to make sure that everything runs smoothly. I always marvelled at the commitment and efficiency of the groups of volunteers running the water tables. The London Marathon causes huge disruption in the communities through which it runs, and absorbs huge amounts of voluntary labour, but hardly anyone minds.

The very different 'Run to the Beat', a half marathon organised by a profit-generating company, attracted no community support, and eventually it had to leave Greenwich, even though each individual runner was raising money for charity. The gift-nature of the London Marathon continues to generate significant community generosity, whereas 'Run to the Beat', designed to raise money for shareholders, generated rejection.

Another example of generous gift is the UK's National Health Service. This too attracts vast amounts of voluntary labour, and thousands of people give blood for no payment.[8] The lesson from the NHS and the London Marathon is that altruism inspires altruism; gift inspires gift; generosity inspires generosity:[9] and the effects of the original gift continue to generate new gifts and new gift relationships, somewhat in contrast to the more short-term nature of contractual activity.[10] A Citizen's Basic Income would have the same effect. Its character as a generous gift would inspire significant amounts of caring and voluntary activity, as well as co-operative enterprises, education, training, and much else.

As Philip Wogaman puts the argument from God's grace to our invited response:

> The whole point of economics is to create and maintain the material conditions which best serve [our] true humanity.

When the latter is subordinated to the former, when [our] integrity and … social relationships are turned into instruments of production, then economic life destroys rather than fulfils our spiritual destiny. To the Christian … this must be understood in terms of God's acts of creation and grace. Through these acts, [we have] been given freedom and the ground to stand upon. Christian response to what God has done involves gratitude and creative service. It involves the attempt to cooperate with God so as to fashion a world more and more hospitable to the covenant community … which is God's intention.[11]

If 'grace' is at the root and centre of the Christian tradition, then a society will be 'Christian' to the extent that it is a grace-centred society, that is, a society that forms its social policy on the basis of grace, on the basis of unconditional giving. From an entirely secular standpoint Richard Titmuss made the same point in his *The Gift Relationship*,[12] in which he calls for social policy to be modelled on the UK's entirely voluntary blood donation scheme: individuals giving blood for no payment, and having no idea to whom the blood will be given; and the NHS giving blood as a gift to whoever needs it. For social policy in the UK to be modelled on the centrality of grace we shall require both education and healthcare to continue to be free at the point of use; we shall need to keep Child Benefit in its unconditional, non-means-tested form; and we shall need a Citizen's Basic Income: not only because it is the most efficient way to eradicate poverty and to create an economy within which individuals can take responsibility for themselves and their dependents, but also because it is the best way to express the grace that is at the heart of Christian theology.

Kathryn Tanner, in her *Economy of Grace*, understands grace to be at the heart of the Christian Gospel:

God does not give gifts to us because of what we have done to deserve them. They are not payments for services rendered.

They are not owed by the fulfilment of some prior condition … .[13]

Throughout her book, Tanner looks for 'points of relevant intersection and intervention'[14] between the economy and the Christian Gospel, so that the economy can be modelled on 'unconditional giving' without the normal ways in which the economy works being dismantled.[15] In relation to social security benefits, she wants to see 'welfare provision as a universal entitlement' – but then unfortunately she contradicts herself by adding 'sensitive only to need'.[16] She wants to see 'gone … all the debasing conditions for receipt of public assistance, the demeaning supervision and invasions of privacy',[17] but clearly does not realise that 'demeaning supervision and invasions of privacy' are intrinsic to the assessment of need. Her theological instincts are absolutely right – that 'unconditional giving' and therefore 'universal giving'[18] should be at the heart of the economy: but she has found herself unable to transfer her theological insights to her understanding of the benefits system. One possible reason for this is that she works in the USA, where unconditional benefits are in rather short supply. Perhaps if she had lived and worked in the UK then she would have understood the NHS and Child Benefit as practical examples of welfare provision modelled on grace, on 'unconditional giving', and would have asked for a Citizen's Basic Income as a natural extension of those provisions. As it is, she cannot conceive of a welfare state modelled on genuine unconditionality: on an 'unconditional giving' that takes no account of need. A genuinely unconditional Citizen's Basic Income, that is, one *not* sensitive to need, would not only reflect the grace of God, but it would fulfil Tanner's other requirement: that a grace-shaped economy should cohere with the way in which the economy actually works.

A Citizen's Basic Income would fit the current needs of our society and economy at least as closely as it would fit the unconditional giving at the heart of the Christian Gospel. New information and communication technology is driving rapid social and economic change, causing severe difficulties for employees and for their families. And, as Thomas Piketty has shown,[19] the return on capital is increasing faster than the growth of the economy, so the gap between wages and the proceeds of productivity is increasing. Less of the proceeds from production is now going back into industry through the payment of wages and the consumption that those wages generate. The consequences are more people on low pay, means-tested benefits filling the gap between wages and subsistence needs, and manufacturing and service industries suffering contractions in demand. Increasing automation – including automation of occupations that we never thought would suffer from it, such as lawyers and lecturers – means that we shall have to find a way of recycling the proceeds of production back into the community so that people can have the resources that they need. A Citizen's Basic Income would achieve this. Initially, a Citizen's Basic Income will need to be funded through changes to the current tax and benefits system, but if it is to be a mechanism that recycles the proceeds of production back into household incomes, then it will have to be paid for by other means as well, such as a higher tax on profits, or a higher tax on dividends. The income-work link that has characterised our work ethic for so long – a link with its own roots in the Christian tradition[20] – will need to be broken. A new grace-shaped ethic is required: society making a gift of an income to every individual, and every one of us making a willing contribution of time, energy and skills to the many kinds of work that our society needs to have done. A Citizen's Basic Income would not be a reward for work done, but rather an income that would enable us to work.

The other side of that coin is that a Citizen's Basic Income would also be an invitation to experience leisure: something increasingly difficult to come by for employees whose employers can keep them attached to their employment twenty-four hours a day through their smartphones.

The creation account in Genesis culminates in leisure:

> Thus the heavens and the earth were finished, and all their multitude. And on the seventh day God finished the work

that he had done, and he rested on the seventh day from all
the work that he had done. So God blessed the seventh day
and hallowed it, because on it God rested from all the work
that he had done in creation.[21]

Leisure is the 'hinge' of the Ten Commandments, providing the
link between those commandments that relate to honouring God
and those that relate to our relationships with each other:

> Remember the sabbath day, and keep it holy. For six days
> you shall labour and do all your work. But the seventh day is
> a sabbath to the Lord your God; you shall not do any work
> – you, your son or your daughter, your male or female slave,
> your livestock, or the alien resident in your towns. For in six
> days the Lord made heaven and earth, the sea, and all that is
> in them, but rested the seventh day; therefore the Lord blessed
> the sabbath day and consecrated it.[22]

Jesus rejected those accretions to this commandment that had
turned the Sabbath into an onerous and dehumanising obligation,
and he reaffirmed the Sabbath as a gift of God, as an aspect of grace:

> The sabbath was made for humankind, and not humankind
> for the Sabbath.[23]

As the commandment makes clear, both work and leisure are
required: 'for six days you shall labour ... the seventh day is a
Sabbath to the Lord your God; you shall not do any work'. We
need both work and leisure, and both of them are gifts from God.

A Citizen's Basic Income recognises all of this. There will be few
people who will wish to survive entirely on the level of Citizen's
Basic Income that is likely to be paid in the near future, but there
will be some that will. That is not a problem. There will be plenty
of people who will want to do the work that society needs to
have done, because the fact that their Citizen's Basic Income will
not be withdrawn as their earnings rise will provide far more of

an incentive than our current out-of-work and in-work benefits, which are withdrawn as earnings rise, and so result in little gain in disposable income as earned income rises. And for many people their Citizen's Basic Income will offer additional employment options. Part-time work will be more viable for many, and the financial security that a Citizen's Basic Income would provide will make highly flexible employment arrangements much safer for those individuals and households for whom such flexibility might be welcome. As employment became more evenly shared, leisure would become a positive opportunity for creative activity rather than a rare opportunity to recharge batteries ready for the next stint of employment in a job that they cannot refuse. The additional leisure that many people might experience would be used for caring, for creativity, for voluntary and community activity, and simply for enjoying life. This is what God intended by the gift of the Sabbath.

Only by breaking the link between work and income shall we be able to understand the created order as a gift of God to be cherished, and as the means by which God provides the wealth that we need. As Paul puts it in relation to spiritual wealth:

> If it is by grace, it is no longer on the basis of works, otherwise grace would no longer be grace.[24]

Our present economic system – which divides us into people who earn an income, and people who receive a grudging and disempowering handout – persuades us that wealth is of a particular monetised kind; that some of us create wealth, and some of us do not; that those who do not create it are to be given as little of it as possible; and that leisure is a guilty distraction from obligated employment. Only when we share a common and secure source of income shall we be able to grasp the fact that wealth belongs to God, that work of all kinds is a response to God's gift of wealth, and that leisure is as much a gift and a requirement as work is.

The archetypal act of grace is the incarnation:

> In the beginning was the Word, and the Word was with God,
> and the Word was God. ... And the Word became flesh and
> lived among us, and we have seen his glory, the glory as of a
> father's only son, full of grace and truth ... From his fullness
> we have all received, grace upon grace.[25]

God has lived a human life, becoming 'incarnate', enfleshed, and
suffering the pain and death that that entails. Nothing will ever
compare with this act of grace: but some actions can be closer
to it than others. The institution that gets closest to it has to
be a Citizen's Basic Income. It is pure grace, a transparent and
unconditional gift, 'full of grace and truth ... grace upon grace'.

The Christian tradition has shaped many of the world's nations,
and particularly the UK: but if it is to continue to do so then we
must not allow that tradition to become merely a set of values
(however virtuous those values might be), nor simply a set of beliefs
and religious practices (even though those must remain central
to the Christian Faith): we must constantly return to the heart of
the Christian Gospel, rebuild the Christian tradition on the basis
of grace, and offer the grace-shaped insights of that tradition as
a contribution to the rebuilding of our society. A significant way
of doing that would be for Christians to contribute to the debate
about Citizen's Basic Income. There is no other social policy that
could claim to be so closely modelled on the grace of God.

3.

Citizen's Basic Income would recognise our individuality

Are not two sparrows sold for a penny? Yet not one of them will fall to the ground unperceived by your Father. And even the hairs of your head are all counted. So do not be afraid; you are of more value than many sparrows.

(Matthew 10:29–31)

Every individual is precious to God: not as a member of a collective, but as an individual. Of course, the New Testament recognises that individuals belong within nations, communities, and families: but Jesus relativised the family by telling his hearers that 'whoever does the will of God is my brother and sister and mother',[1] and for him it was the coming Kingdom of God that was the collective that mattered, and not the social arrangements of the day. We are distinct individuals, and each of us is responsible for our own decisions:[2] so it is appropriate that Citizen's Basic Income should be paid to individuals, and not to households. The individual would then be able to choose to whom to relate, what work to do, and how to organise their life.

This is not, as might be thought, an attack on families. It is current means-tested benefits that are bad for families. Means-tested benefits are usually paid to households, and not to individuals; and the total amount paid to a couple will generally be lower than the two individuals would receive in total if they were claiming benefits separately. The argument generally offered in favour of this approach that it is cheaper for two people to live together than for individuals to live separately, so individuals living with other individuals need less money than individuals living alone. Where only the poorest are claiming a particular benefit, and wealthier people are paying for it, there will be pressure for the Government to reduce costs by restricting benefits – and the economies of scale generated by people living together are an easy target. But such a system generates some significant problems. A lone parent on means-tested benefits who moves in with someone else will lose their independent income. The outcome is a benefits system that can make it financially beneficial for parents to live apart, and one that provides no incentive for people to live together. A Citizen's Basic Income would continue to be paid at the same rate, whether someone lived on their own or with others, and so would not disincentivise people moving in with each other. This does not mean that a Citizen's Basic Income would incentivise coupledom. Because each individual's Citizen's Basic Income would never change, whatever relationships they were in, and whatever kind of household they lived in, no particular relationship type or household arrangement would be either incentivised or disincentivised. In relation to the current system, moving to a benefits system based on Citizen's Basic Income would mean a larger number of permanent relationships, simply because the current system disincentivises them. The effect on the housing crisis could be significant.

A particularly problematic characteristic of current means-tested benefits systems is that they take into account the earnings of a spouse's or partner's earnings when calculating a household's benefits. If one member of a couple becomes unemployed, their contributory unemployment benefit (in the UK, their Contribution-based Jobseeker's Allowance) will soon run out, and they will have to claim means-tested unemployment benefit (in the UK, Income-based Jobseeker's Allowance). Apart from a small earnings disregard, their benefits will be reduced by the amount of their spouse's earnings. There will then be little financial incentive for the spouse or partner to continue to earn: and, if it looks as if their spouse's or partner's unemployment might last for some time, they might decide not to continue in paid employment. It is therefore no surprise that Richard Berthoud has identified a long term trend towards 'work-rich' and 'work-poor' households: towards a growing number of two-earner households, and a growing number of no-earner households – although this latter trend now appears to have levelled off. In 2007 he wrote that

> there has been a steep increase … in the number of non-working adults without a partner, or whose partner does not have a job. The proportion has doubled from 7 per cent to 14 per cent over 30 years. Most of these 'work-poor' families live on social security benefits, and have very low incomes.[3]

Entirely different behaviour would be generated if a Citizen's Basic Income were to replace means-tested benefits. Whatever happened to someone's employment or earned income, no household member's Citizen's Basic Income would change. There would therefore be far less of a disincentive for the partner of someone who became unemployed to give up their employment. Each party would be able to behave as an individual, rather than as a member of a couple subject to a joint means-tested benefit claim. Even in these days of professed equality, there might still be psychological pressure felt by a woman to give up her employment if her husband became unemployed, but the fact that her earnings would continue to support the family financially, and would not reduce the man's Citizen's Basic Income, would substantially reduce that pressure, and would be a significant incentive for the man to seek employment or self-employment.

We can therefore see that Citizen's Basic Income, by treating people as individuals, would be good for such families. It would be good for other families, too. In a family claiming in-work means-tested benefits, a single claim has to be made. The partner making the claim has to know all of the financial details of the other partner, and they don't need to know the financial details of the one making the claim. This is discriminatory. The UK's Income

Tax is assessed on the basis of the individual, and one partner does not need to know the financial details of the other. The same situation should apply in the benefits field – and, with a Citizen's Basic Income, it would.

Because each individual would be paid their own Citizen's Basic Income, and because no circumstances relating to anyone else would change it, the household's Citizen's Basic Incomes would not interfere in any way with decisions relating to relationships or employment patterns: so for the first time these could be decided entirely on the basis of far more relevant criteria, such as the needs of a family's children, or the employment pattern most suited to a couple's chosen lifestyle. Perhaps counterintuitively, treating everyone as an individual would be good for families.

A Citizen's Basic Income would also recognise our individuality in the workplace. Someone currently on means-tested in-work benefits (such as the UK's so-called 'Working Tax Credits', and, in the future, its so-called 'Universal Credit') will find that if their wages go up then their benefits will go down. Equally damaging, someone not in employment can find themselves subject to a sanctions regime if they do not seek employment in the prescribed manner. They can find a training course rudely interrupted by an instruction to take a full-time job when a part-time one would be more appropriate; or they can find their benefits stopped if they decline an offer of employment and continue with a course that will provide them with the skills that will need if they are to enter an occupation in need of skilled workers. The individual is not regarded as free to form a contract with an employer if they choose to do so. They are treated as a cog in a machine, rather than as an individual with choices to make. A Citizen's Basic Income, which would continue at the same rate whatever someone's employment or training circumstances, would change all of this. The individual would be truly a responsible adult individual, able to make decisions without interference. Young people would be able to choose part-time or occasional employment that would fit round their degree or training course, and their Citizen's Basic Income and wages would together enable them to reduce or eliminate student debt.

Parents and other carers would be able to seek the employment pattern that suited them; and people approaching retirement would be able to scale back their employment so that retirement would no longer be the emotional and financial shock that it so often is.

The effect would be similar in relation to opportunities for voluntary work, the fulfilment of caring obligations, and the pursuit of political and other vocations. For many people, their Citizen's Basic Income would provide the opportunity to cut their hours of employment in order to spend more time caring for the local nature reserve, to spend more time caring for a disabled relative, or to pursue a political career. No longer would unpaid internships, with all of the social and career advantages that they offer, be available only to the wealthy.

For many, the important change would relate to their employment or self-employment. No longer would additional earnings result in little financial gain, so they might seek new skills, pursue a new career, contribute additional finances to their family, contribute newly gained skills to their new profession, or contribute greater social capital to their community. So yet again, and again somewhat counterintuitively, being treated as an individual could enhance our engagement with our families, our communities, and our society.

In the workplace, in the family, in our communities, and in our society, to replace means-tested benefits with a Citizen's Basic Income would for the first time turn all of us into individuals with the value ascribed by Jesus' words, and would set us free to choose how to form and serve families, how to serve our communities, and how to benefit our society. Jesus' words encourage us to see every individual as having a unique and infinite value. A Citizen's Basic Income would do the same.

Citizen's Basic Income would recognise God's equal treatment of us

The kingdom of heaven is like a landowner who went out early in the morning to hire labourers for his vineyard. After agreeing with the labourers for the usual daily wage, he sent them into his vineyard. When he went out about nine o'clock, he saw others standing idle in the market-place; and he said to them, 'You also go into the vineyard, and I will pay you whatever is right.' So they went. When he went out again about noon and about three o'clock, he did the same. And about five o'clock he went out and found others standing around; and he said to them, 'Why are you standing here idle all day?' They said to him, 'Because no one has hired us.' He said to them, 'You also go into the vineyard.' When evening came, the owner of the vineyard said to his manager, 'Call the labourers and give them their pay, beginning with the last and then going to the first.' When those hired about five o'clock came, each of them received the usual daily wage. Now when the first came, they thought they would receive more; but each of them also received the usual daily wage. And when they received it, they grumbled against the landowner, saying, 'These last worked only one hour, and you have made them equal to us who have borne the burden of the day and the scorching heat.' But he replied to one of them, 'Friend, I am doing you no wrong; did you not agree with me for the usual daily wage? Take what belongs to you and go; I choose to give to this last

the same as I give to you. Am I not allowed to do what I
choose with what belongs to me? Or are you envious because I
am generous?' So the last will be first, and the first will be last.
(Matthew 20:1–16)

I have quoted this parable in full because it is important to hear the whole of Jesus' parable of the workers in the vineyard. But what's it about? Is Jesus espousing the socialist doctrine 'to each according to their need, from each according to their ability'? Or is it about God's welcome of society's outcasts into the Kingdom of God alongside the Pharisees and Sadducees, who have spent their lives conforming to the Jewish Law, and about the Pharisees' and Sadducees' disgruntlement when Jesus makes it clear that that's the way it is? Was the parable remembered because it represented the equal welcome of Gentiles into membership of the Church after the initial phase in which the Church had been composed entirely of Jews? Or perhaps all three of these meanings constitute the parable's meaning?

Whatever the parable meant to its first hearers, and whatever it meant to the earliest Christians, one thing is clear: this parable is not a description of completely unmerited generosity. Only those who do at least *some* work in the vineyard get paid. So this is a parable about God's equal treatment of every one of us, whatever our contribution. The vineyard represents the nation of Israel, as it always did in Jesus' parables.[1] In a real vineyard, the only people present are the workers, and they will be working: so the occupants of the vineyard in Jesus' parable had to be workers, and they had to be working. It is in that context that the vineyard owner is generous, paying them all the same, however hard they had worked.

We are all made 'in the image of God',[2] and so share a fundamental God-given equality. Christians eventually understood that this implied equal freedom for every human being,[3] and therefore the abolition of slavery. In our day, the belief that we are all made in the image of God could inspire an equally world-changing innovation: a Citizen's Basic Income – not an equal total income for every individual (which would not be practical, nor would it prove to be desirable), but an equal financial platform on which individuals would be able to build unequally. God 'makes his sun rise on the evil and on the good, and sends rain on the righteous and on the unrighteous'.[4] We possess a foundational equality: one that promises equality in the Kingdom of God, and one that invites us to create signposts to that final equality: signposts such as a Citizen's Basic Income.

Eight centuries before Jesus' time, the prophet Amos prescribed judgement on the inequality in Israel:

> because you trample on the poor
> and take from them levies of grain,
> you have built houses of hewn stone,
> but you shall not live in them;
> you have planted pleasant vineyards,
> but you shall not drink their wine.[5]

> I will tear down the winter house as well as the summer house;
> and the houses of ivory shall perish,
> and the great houses shall come to an end,
> says the Lord.[6]

Jesus is likely to have known these passages from the prophet Amos; and he might also have heard his mother Mary sing the somewhat revolutionary song that we find in Luke's gospel:

> He has shown strength with his arm;
> he has scattered the proud in the thoughts of their hearts.
> He has brought down the powerful from their thrones,
> and lifted up the lowly;
> he has filled the hungry with good things,
> and sent the rich away empty.[7]

The perfect tense here is one of prophetic certainty: that is, it is so certain that God will keep the promise expressed here that it is as if it has already happened.

Our current social structures and social security provisions fail to provide a foundational equality, or even equality of opportunity, let alone an equal outcome. There was a brief period following the Second World War when inequality in many developed countries began to diminish: but the past thirty years have seen increasing inequality. An increasing understanding that inequality is bad both for our society and for the economy has generated little effort to rein in the growing inequality.[8] No Christian can put up with this.[9] Our creation in God's image, Jesus' parables, and Jesus' valuing of those whom the society of his day did not value, lay an obligation on anyone who follows Jesus to work for deeper equality, and perhaps for the kind of reversal promised in Mary's song.

In his letter to the Church in Galatia, Paul told them that

> there is no longer Jew or Greek, there is no longer slave or free, there is no longer male and female; for all of you are one in Christ Jesus.[10]

Expressed rather differently, we find the same conviction in the letter of James:

> My brothers and sisters, do you with your acts of favouritism really believe in our glorious Lord Jesus Christ? For if a person with gold rings and in fine clothes comes into your assembly, and if a poor person in dirty clothes also comes in, and if you take notice of the one wearing the fine clothes and say, 'Have a seat here, please', while to the one who is poor you say, 'Stand there', or, 'Sit at my feet', have you not made distinctions among yourselves, and become judges with evil thoughts? Listen, my beloved brothers and sisters. Has not God chosen the poor in the world to be rich in faith and to be heirs of the kingdom that he has promised to those who love him?[11]

And in relation to financial provision, Paul expected the Churches to work towards greater equality:

> I do not mean that there should be relief for others and pressure on you, but it is a question of a fair balance between your present abundance and their need, so that their abundance may be for your need, in order that there may be a fair balance.[12]

Because there will be no inequality in the Kingdom of God, there is to be no inequality in the Church. The earliest Christians had no opportunity to work for change in the social fabric of their day: all they could do was represent the character of the coming Kingdom of God within the life of the Church. It was on this basis that Paul appealed to Philemon to give his slave Onesimus his freedom. They were brothers in Christ, and their master/slave relationship contradicted that foundational equality.[13] In our day Christians are more able to work for change in the world in which we live, so these passages, which laid an obligation on early Christians to fashion the life of the Church according to the equality promised in the Kingdom of God, lay on us an obligation to fashion the life of our society according to that same equality – which means in particular that we have an obligation to work for a welfare state more in tune with the character of the Kingdom of God.[14]

One Christian social policy academic who attempted this was R. H. Tawney. For him, equality was at the heart of the Kingdom of God, and therefore needed to be at the heart of our society:

> Those who dread a dead-level of income or wealth, which is not at the moment a very pressing danger in England, do not dread, it seems, a dead-level of law and order, and of security for life and property.[15]

As Daniel Jenkins has pointed out, God's love for each of us, equal and unique, needs to find expression in experienced equality, and not only in an ascribed human equality. Jenkins suggests that the equality that we need to experience is equal opportunity to seek excellence, and that this requires an adequate income, although not necessarily 'a dead-level of income'.[16] What equality of opportunity does require, though, is an equally secure income for everyone. Our current income maintenance system does not deliver that. Both earned income and benefits income are less secure than they were. The only secure income in the UK at the moment is Child Benefit. To base an income for adults on the unconditionality and therefore the security of Child Benefit would begin to provide the kind of secure income that equality of opportunity requires. An abstract citizenship is not enough:[17] what is required is the kind of economic citizenship that a Citizen's Basic Income would provide.

As Jesus puts it in his Sermon on the Mount:

> You have heard that it was said, 'You shall love your neighbour and hate your enemy.' But I say to you, Love your enemies and pray for those who persecute you, so that you may be children of your Father in heaven; for he makes his sun rise on the evil and on the good, and sends rain on the righteous and on the unrighteous.[18]

The Kingdom of God will be characterised by God's equal treatment of all of us. We are invited to live in that Kingdom now, to experience God's equal treatment, and to respond by seeking a society in which everyone is treated equally. The least we can do is argue for a small equal income for every member of society: a Citizen's Basic Income.

5.

Citizen's Basic Income would provide for the poor

*When the Son of Man comes in his glory, and all the angels
with him, then he will sit on the throne of his glory. All the
nations will be gathered before him, and he will separate
people one from another as a shepherd separates the sheep from
the goats, and he will put the sheep at his right hand and the
goats at the left. Then the king will say to those at his right
hand, 'Come, you that are blessed by my Father, inherit the
kingdom prepared for you from the foundation of the world;
for I was hungry and you gave me food, I was thirsty and
you gave me something to drink, I was a stranger and you
welcomed me, I was naked and you gave me clothing, I was
sick and you took care of me, I was in prison and you visited
me.' Then the righteous will answer him, 'Lord, when was it
that we saw you hungry and gave you food, or thirsty and
gave you something to drink? And when was it that we saw
you a stranger and welcomed you, or naked and gave you
clothing? And when was it that we saw you sick or in prison
and visited you?' And the king will answer them, 'Truly I
tell you, just as you did it to one of the least of these who are
members of my family, you did it to me.'*

(Matthew 25:31–40)

In this parable in Matthew's gospel Jesus clearly regards feeding and
clothing the poor as an essential task for his followers. When early

in his ministry in Galilee he went to the synagogue in Nazareth and was invited to read from the books of the prophets, he read from the prophet Isaiah:

> The Spirit of the Lord is upon me,
> because he has anointed me
> to bring good news to the poor.
> He has sent me to proclaim release to the captives
> and recovery of sight to the blind,
> to let the oppressed go free,
> to proclaim the year of the Lord's favour.[1]

– and he followed the reading with the statement that 'today this scripture has been fulfilled in your hearing'.[2] The Kingdom of God – which would be particularly good news for the poor – had 'come near'.[3] So now it is still 'near', and Jesus' followers continue to have a responsibility to feed and clothe the poor as a sign of the Kingdom's coming.

The Old Testament, too, is full of the expectation that the people of Israel will feed the poor. When they collected in their harvests they were to leave sufficient for the poor to collect:[4] a command that seems to have been kept.[5] If a cloak was taken as surety for a debt, it was to be returned in the evening to ensure that the debtor did not get cold during the night:[6] which presumably meant the cloak changing hands twice a day until the debt was paid. Alongside all of this interest in ensuring that the poor were fed and clothed, the Jewish Law was intent on maintaining the dignity of the poor. 'You shall not render an unjust judgement; you shall not be partial to the poor or defer to the great: with justice you shall judge your neighbour'.[7] In relation to the law, the poor person was to be treated in exactly the same way as the rich, and the rich in the same way as the poor.

This was Jesus' heritage when he came to shape his own words and behaviour: which means that it is our heritage, too. We, too, need to feed and clothe the poor, bring good news to the poor, and treat the rich and the poor alike, thus maintaining the dignity of the poor as made in the image of God:

> God said, 'Let us make humankind in our image, according to our likeness; and let them have dominion over the fish of the sea, and over the birds of the air, and over the cattle, and over all the wild animals of the earth, and over every creeping thing that creeps upon the earth.' So God created humankind in his image, in the image of God he created them; male and female he created them.[8]

This verse from Psalm 8 is about all of us, and not just about some:

> Yet you have made them a little lower than God,
> and crowned them with glory and honour.[9]

Means-tested benefits that stigmatise their recipients grant no recognition to our status as made in God's image and as possessing a dignity bettered only by God's. A Citizen's Basic Income would recognise our status in a way that no other social security benefit can. It would come without bureaucratic interference in our lives, without categorising us, and without dividing off its recipients from people who do not receive benefits.

The question 'How should we as Christians ensure that the poor are fed and clothed, and are provided with all of the other necessities of life in the society in which they live?' looks at first sight as if it has an obvious answer: 'We need to give money to the poor, and when they don't have any money we should ensure that they have food and clothes'. It often feels natural for Christians and Church leaders to argue for increases in the levels of means-tested benefits, to argue against cuts in benefits, and to organise foodbanks. At first sight, the suggestion that we should give money to everyone would not seem to be the answer required: for surely, it is the poor that need money, not the rich. But however counterintuitive it might be, to give money to everyone really is the answer.

To address first of all the situation in developed countries: to give money only to the poor requires us to take that money away as soon as someone ceases to be poor. So a poor person who finds a job, or who increases their initially low income, finds their benefits being reduced, and they might at the same time find themselves paying income tax, other deductions, and fares to work: so they remain poor. The answer to this difficulty would appear to be to allow them to keep their benefits for a while: but that would set up an injustice, because someone who had not been on those benefits, and was on the same wages, would be worse off than the person who had been on benefits and had been allowed to keep them. The only answer is to give money to everyone, and to allow everyone to keep it, whatever happens to their earnings.

When forty years ago I worked in Brixton's Supplementary Benefit office for two years, administering means-tested benefits, I was interested to discover that the most popular benefit among the poorest people was Child Benefit: a payment that went to everyone, including the rich. The reason for Child Benefit's popularity was that it was never taken away. Someone who was on out-of-work means-tested benefits who took a job for a few hours a week would find their benefits stopped, their benefits recalculated, and their benefits restarted at a lower level – and, if they were lucky, with the correct back-payments. Their family budget would be thrown into chaos: but their Child Benefit would keep on coming. It really didn't matter to them that the richest people in the land received Child Benefit (after all, they were paying far more in Income Tax than they would ever receive in Child Benefit). What mattered was that their own Child Benefit would never stop as long as they were caring for children. An additional reason for Child Benefit being so popular was that it went to everyone, so there was absolutely no stigma attached to it. There was of course plenty of stigma attached to means-tested benefits, and there still is.

As we have seen, it is as important that the poor should be treated in the same way as everyone else as that the poor should be fed and clothed. The only way to achieve this is to model our benefits system on Child Benefit and to pay to everyone enough to live on, whatever their other income. If initially we cannot afford to do this then we should at least make a start and pay a small unconditional income to every individual – a Citizen's Basic Income – and then work hard to increase it.

Again counterintuitively, it is equally important that the poor should be taxed in the same way as everyone else. The UK is in the process of raising the Income Tax Personal Allowance. This might at first sight look like a good idea – but it isn't. First of all, if the higher thresholds are raised by the same amount at the same time, then raising the Personal Allowance gives more to the rich than to the poor, because the rich benefit by the additional personal allowance multiplied by their highest tax rate, while the poor benefit only by the additional personal allowance multiplied by the basic rate – a fact never mentioned when government ministers say that they are 'taking the lowest earners out of income tax'. Secondly, paying Income Tax generates political engagement – because we might be interested in what the government is doing with the tax that we pay: so to take the poorest out of paying tax is to reduce their political engagement. (The more cynical among us might have noticed that in the UK a Conservative Government, helped by Liberal Democrats in the last parliament, were removing the poorest people from paying income tax, and thus reducing the political engagement of individuals who were more likely to have been Labour voters.[10])

In order to ensure that the poor are fed and clothed, and at the same time that everyone is treated the same, we need to pay to everyone of the same age a Citizen's Basic Income of the same amount; and we need everyone who is earning a living to pay income tax.

But what of developing countries? Isn't their situation different? No, it isn't. Some highly successful pilot projects in Namibia and India have shown that to pay a small Citizen's Basic Income can have a considerable impact on poverty, mainly by stimulating economic activity among the families with the lowest net incomes.[11] And, as in developed countries, to pay a Citizen's Basic Income is to treat everyone the same, and is thus to maintain every individual's dignity. In crisis situations aid agencies will still need to provide food and shelter, but under normal circumstances the needs of the poor will be best served by providing every individual in a community with the same amount of money and then allowing them to use it to provide the services that they need. The pilot projects have shown that every community is perfectly capable of doing that.

So far we have avoided any discussion of whether we should be more concerned about absolute poverty than relative poverty, and I shall continue to avoid that question.[12] However, I *shall* discuss the question as to whether poverty is best seen as a static or as a dynamic reality. As Ruth Lister has suggested, poverty is as much a process as a state, and what matters most to a poor family is the ability to leave the poverty into which they have been plunged.[13] To take an example: a family with a net income of £15,000 per annum that can raise their net income to £20,000 per annum by earning an additional £7,000 might be counted as better off than a family with a net income of £17,000 per annum that can only raise its net income to £18,000 per annum if it earns an additional £7,000 per annum. The marginal deduction rate – the proportion of additional earnings that is withdrawn through benefits withdrawal and tax payments – really matters. A Citizen's Basic Income of any amount would reduce the marginal deduction rate of any family on means-tested in-work or out-of-work benefits: and in terms of poverty understood as a process, a Citizen's Basic Income of any size would be worth more to a family on benefits than an increase in the level of their means-tested benefits.

We can now clear up a common confusion. It is often said – by Christian economists,[14] as well as by politicians – that giving money to the poor is not the answer to poverty. This statement is usually based on an assumption that the only benefits payable to the poor are means-tested ones: and it is true that giving money to the poor in the form of means-tested benefits is not an answer to poverty. If the poor – and everyone else – were to receive unconditional incomes, then the answer would of course be very different. Unconditional benefits would be a very effective answer to poverty. It will always be true, of course, that poverty has many roots: poor housing, poor health, addictions, unemployment, broken families, insufficient educational opportunities, and so on; and all of these need to be tackled: but it is also true that unconditional benefits can both relieve poverty and at the same time create a ladder out of poverty.[15] The statement 'giving money to the poor is not an answer to poverty' is only true in relation to means-tested benefits. It is definitely not true in relation to unconditional ones.

Here I must add a note of caution: Citizen's Basic Income will never come alone. It will always be accompanied by changes that need to be made elsewhere in the tax and benefits system in order to pay for everyone's Citizen's Basic Incomes. If no additional public expenditure is available then the money to pay for Citizen's Basic Incomes will need to come from reducing income tax allowances, reducing or abolishing existing benefits, and maybe increasing income tax rates. For any given Citizen's Basic Income level there will be a wide diversity of possible Citizen's Basic Income *schemes*: that is, combinations of tax allowance reductions, tax rates increases, and benefits revisions. The complexity of the current tax and benefits systems can mean that, at the point of implementation of a Citizen's Basic Income scheme, some households could find themselves worse off: not because there is anything wrong with a Citizen's Basic Income, but because of the way in which the current system operates. Clearly it would be unacceptable for a Citizen's Basic Income scheme to reduce the disposable incomes of households already suffering from low disposable incomes; and it would also be unacceptable if a Citizen's Basic Income scheme were to exacerbate existing inequalities. Only careful research will ensure that any Citizen's Basic Income scheme that we implement will redistribute from rich to poor, and will not impose losses on low income households at the point of implementation.[16]

Jesus' parable of the sheep and the goats, quoted at the beginning of this chapter, goes on to hold to account those who did not feed the hungry:

'... for I was hungry and you gave me no food, I was thirsty and you gave me nothing to drink, I was a stranger and you did not welcome me, naked and you did not give me clothing, sick and in prison and you did not visit me.' Then they also will answer, 'Lord, when was it that we saw you hungry or thirsty or a stranger or naked or sick or in prison, and did not take care of you?' Then he will answer them, 'Truly I tell you, just as you did not do it to one of the least of these, you did not do it to me.'[17]

We therefore have a solemn obligation to ensure that any Citizen's Basic Income scheme that we implement does not leave anyone already on a low income in a worse financial position than they are now. Fortunately it is entirely possible to achieve a Citizen's Basic Income scheme that imposes negligible losses on low income households, and that redistributes slightly from rich to poor.[18]

In the Letter of James, we find both the requirement to treat everyone equally:

For if a person with gold rings and in fine clothes comes into your assembly, and if a poor person in dirty clothes also comes in, and if you take notice of the one wearing the fine clothes and say, 'Have a seat here, please', while to the one who is poor you say, 'Stand there', or, 'Sit at my feet', have you not made distinctions among yourselves, and become judges with evil thoughts?[19]

– and the requirement to respond to the needs of the poor:

What good is it, my brothers and sisters, if you say you have faith but do not have works? Can faith save you? If a brother or sister is naked and lacks daily food, and one of you says to them, 'Go in peace; keep warm and eat your fill', and yet you do not supply their bodily needs, what is the good of that? So faith by itself, if it has no works, is dead ... a person is justified by works and not by faith alone.[20]

Christians have an obligation to tackle poverty, and at the same time to maintain the dignity of the poor and the equal value of every child of God. While it might be counterintuitive for Christians to argue that every member of society – including the rich – should be given a regular income by the state, it would appear that this would be the best approach. To pay to every member of society an unconditional and nonwithdrawable income – a Citizen's Basic Income – would reduce poverty in the way that would most effectively maintain the dignity of every member of society.

6.

A Citizen's Basic Income would not judge

Do not judge, and you will not be judged; do not condemn, and you will not be condemned.

(Luke 6:37)

Jesus did not judge: 'I do not judge anyone who hears my words and does not keep them, for I came not to judge the world, but to save the world.'[1] Lots of people clearly experienced judgement when they found themselves in Jesus' presence, but that is not the same thing as Jesus judging them. Jesus did not condemn a woman taken in adultery: although she would have gone away from her encounter with Jesus having experienced his command not to sin again. And he did not condemn a swindling tax collector: instead, Zacchaeus freely offered to pay back what he ought not to have taken.[2] Jesus enabled those who encountered him to judge themselves. He did not judge them: so when Jesus commanded us not to judge, he was simply asking us to follow in his footsteps.

However, knowing that Jesus will not judge us for our actions can leave communities with a problem. One of the issues that Paul tackles in his first letter to the Church in Corinth is that of food offered to idols. Christians with 'strong' consciences were perfectly capable of understanding that idols did not represent real gods; that if food was offered to idols before being eaten then nothing had happened to that food, and it was still God's gift to us; and that their consciences could therefore remain entirely clear.

Christians with 'weaker' consciences, however, might believe that
to eat food that had been offered to idols was a denial of their faith
in the God whom they now worshipped – particularly if they had
previously been devotees of the idols in question. They might be
equally concerned that other people might interpret their actions
as a denial of their faith in the God revealed in Jesus Christ. Paul's
instruction to 'the strong' to 'take care that this liberty of yours
does not somehow become a stumbling-block to the weak'[3] was a
recognition that someone with a 'weak' conscience might discover
that another Christian had eaten food that had been offered to
idols, and they might find their conscience 'wounded'.[4] It is
then the 'strong' Christian who is judged, not the 'weak' Christian.
The 'strong' Christian is not to judge the 'weak' Christian: rather,
the 'strong' Christian is not to eat meat offered to idols in case the
'weak' Christian is 'destroyed' by their doing so.[5]

A consistent message emerges from Jesus' words and actions, and
from Paul's letter to the Corinthians: it is not our place to judge
another Christian, but we do have a responsibility to care for other
Christians. The second part of this rule finds support in Jesus' words:

> If any of you put a stumbling-block before one of these
> little ones who believe in me, it would be better for you if a
> great millstone were hung around your neck and you were
> thrown into the sea.[6]

Jesus said this, too:

> Woe to you, scribes and Pharisees, hypocrites! For you tithe
> mint, dill, and cummin, and have neglected the weightier
> matters of the law: justice and mercy and faith. It is these
> you ought to have practised without neglecting the others.[7]

Further woes follow. Matthew's gospel in particular is not short
of Jesus' judgements on the privileged and the hypocritical. It is
the poor and the vulnerable who are not judged, and it is the
privileged who sometimes are. And so Paul does not judge the

'weak' Christian, and tell them that they are wrong: instead, he urges the 'strong' Christian not to scandalise the 'weaker' one, and implies a judgement if they do.

There is plenty of judgement in most countries' benefits systems. Someone is judged to have committed fraud if they have not declared small additional earnings, or if they have not declared that the father of their child moved in with them for a few weeks before going abroad yet again. This contrasts with the leniency with which people are often treated if they have inadvertently or otherwise omitted to mention a source of income on their tax return.

Someone is 'sanctioned' for not turning up for an interview with a civil servant, or for not going to a job interview. Throughout the system there is a pervasive judgement that the claimant is not telling the truth. Whatever the issue, evidence has to be presented: evidence of rent, evidence of identity, evidence of address, evidence of earned income, evidence of savings. This is all rather different from tax systems, in which the taxpayer is generally believed without being asked for evidence. So here it is the more vulnerable who are being judged, and the less vulnerable who are not. If someone has a sizeable unearned income, perhaps from an inheritance, or because they have been fortunate in their share dealings, then no civil servant will ask them to account for the fact that they are not seeking employment.

Most of those who were making the decisions that caused the banks to collapse in 2008 were not only not judged for their actions, but were generously rewarded with government-funded bonuses. The situation is very different for someone with lower earning potential, and with no unearned income, and who is therefore receiving in-work or out-of-work means-tested benefits. They will be judged for not being employed, or for being employed for too few hours.

In the UK, the 1980s saw a spate of 'strivers v. skivers' language, and the last few years have seen a significant revival of it, with politicians referencing the implied division in our society, and the press gladly joining in.[8] There are all kinds of reasons why some people might not be employed: illness, disability, mental illness, lack of skills, caring responsibilities, the closure of their town's only large employer, or simply discouragement in a highly competitive employment market … . No matter: they are skivers. The vulnerable have been judged. The strong, who make their money from closing the factory on which the town had previously relied for employment, are not judged. They are the strivers.

A different but in some ways similar distinction has been drawn since the 1834 Poor Law Reform Bill, which judged between the deserving poor (children, the elderly, people with disabilities) and the undeserving poor (able-bodied working age adults who are not employed):[9] a distinction now shifting as people with disabilities are put through onerous tests to determine their ability to earn a living.

This is all very different from Jesus' judgement of the privileged and his refusal to judge the vulnerable; and different too from Paul's judgement of the 'strong' and his refusal to judge the 'weak'. If anyone is to be judged, then it should be the privileged and the wealthy, some of whom should perhaps be asked what contribution *they* are making to society, and others of whom should be asked about the cost to others of the privileges that they possess. Perhaps there should be health warnings displayed on some family crests, or at the entrances of some of the UK's National Trust properties: This family's wealth, or this magnificent house, was built with the proceeds of slave trading.

All of this raises in a stark way the question as to what kind of benefits system Christians should want to see. Clearly it needs to be one in which the vulnerable are not subject to judgements to which the strong and the wealthy are not subject. No benefits system based on means-tested benefits could fit such a criterion. A contribution-based system might do so, but only if it recognises that the most vulnerable would be unable to contribute, and would therefore need to be 'credited' with contributions: thus turning the contributory system into something very close to a universal one funded by income taxes. The only kind of benefit that would not permit the vulnerable to be judged at all would be a universal benefit such as Child Benefit or Citizen's Basic Income. No sanctions could be attached to it. Everyone would be treated the same: so everyone would be asked for evidence of identity and for bank account details, and no one would be asked for anything else. In one respect an unconditional benefit would not represent Jesus' attitude, because it would not judge the wealthy: but in every other respect it would fit. The important factor is that the vulnerable would not be judged. Just as in the Church 'there is no longer Jew or Greek, there is no longer slave or free, there is no longer male and female; for all of you … are one in Christ Jesus',[10] so in our society there should no longer be 'deserving' or 'undeserving', 'strivers' or 'skivers'. In one sense, of course, we are all undeserving, because we are all sinful human beings:[11] but at the same time we are all equally deserving in relation to God's creation of us in his own image, in relation to the gift of the created order to be used responsibly by all of us, and in relation to God's equal love for us.[12] So there should be no social division based on an ascribed deservingness or undeservingness, because all of us are both: or on whether society counts us as strivers or skivers – for again, all of us are both. No judgements should be made as to who belongs in which category. As Charlesworth and Williams put it:

> Helping the poor is our responsibility; how they respond is theirs. When we actively cultivate biblical attitudes of human dignity, mercy, kindness, compassion, justice, and generosity, our hearts have no place to label any person made in the image of God as undeserving.[13]

It might have been thought that Jesus' judgements and his failures to judge would be a rather barren field in which to search for criteria for a benefits system: but we have found it to be most fruitful. Jesus' failure to judge the vulnerable argues clearly for unconditional and therefore universal benefits. Now all we need is a tax system that judges the wealthy and privileged.

Citizen's Basic Income would constantly forgive

*When he returned to Capernaum after some days, it was
reported that he was at home. So many gathered around
that there was no longer room for them, not even in front of
the door; and he was speaking the word to them. Then some
people came, bringing to him a paralysed man, carried by
four of them. And when they could not bring him to Jesus
because of the crowd, they removed the roof above him; and
after having dug through it, they let down the mat on which
the paralytic lay. When Jesus saw their faith, he said to the
paralytic, 'Son, your sins are forgiven.' Now some of the scribes
were sitting there, questioning in their hearts, 'Why does this
fellow speak in this way? It is blasphemy! Who can forgive
sins but God alone?' At once Jesus perceived in his spirit that
they were discussing these questions among themselves; and
he said to them, 'Why do you raise such questions in your
hearts? Which is easier, to say to the paralytic, "Your sins are
forgiven", or to say, "Stand up and take your mat and walk"?
But so that you may know that the Son of Man has authority
on earth to forgive sins' – he said to the paralytic – 'I say to
you, stand up, take your mat and go to your home.' And he
stood up, and immediately took the mat and went out before
all of them; so that they were all amazed and glorified God,
saying, 'We have never seen anything like this!'*

(Mark 2:1–12)

Forgiveness is complicated, and it is far from easy to discover Jesus' attitude to God's forgiveness of our wrongdoing. In the passage from Mark's gospel, forgiveness is simply offered. There is no conditionality. However, in the prayer that Jesus taught his disciples, we pray that God will

> forgive us our debts,
> as we also have forgiven our debtors.[1]

The forgiveness of debts once every seven years was commanded by the Law,[2] so Jesus' disciples would not have found the conditionality in this prayer an alien concept. Whenever we say the Lord's Prayer, we are *asking* that conditionality should be applied. Jesus follows up the prayer by saying that

> if you forgive others their trespasses, your heavenly Father will also forgive you; but if you do not forgive others, neither will your Father forgive your trespasses.[3]

Jesus told a parable about a master forgiving a servant a huge debt. The servant then has a fellow-servant thrown into jail for not paying a small debt. The master is understandably angry, and throws the servant into jail.[4] Here the reciprocity is complex and bidirectional. God forgives us; in response, we are expected to forgive; and, if we do not, then God's forgiveness is withdrawn. Forgiveness functions as a covenant: God's generosity; our answering generosity; God's anger if our actions do not echo God's forgiveness.

So we have some complexly conditional forgiveness, and also the passage from Mark's gospel in which Jesus simply forgives. He appears to know nothing about the man on the stretcher. Whatever he has done, Jesus has forgiven it.

What are we to make of this combination? Did Jesus change his mind? In the gospel chronologies, both the healing miracle and the prayer that Jesus taught his disciples come near to the beginning of Jesus' ministry: but we cannot conclude that the order in which events are placed in the gospels is the order in which they occurred, so it is perfectly possible that Jesus initially believed that forgiveness was conditional on our forgiving, and then came to believe otherwise; or that he initially thought that forgiveness was simply a gift, and then came to believe that it was conditional. The former transition is the more likely. Jesus appears to have begun as a disciple of John the Baptist.[5] For John, God's forgiveness was highly conditional on repentance and the amendment of life.[6] Then Jesus' and John's ways parted, and significant differences emerged: first of all over lifestyle:

> Now John's disciples and the Pharisees were fasting; and people came and said to him, 'Why do John's disciples and the disciples of the Pharisees fast, but your disciples do not fast?' Jesus said to them, 'The wedding-guests cannot fast while the bridegroom is with them, can they? As long as they have the bridegroom with them, they cannot fast. The days will come when the bridegroom is taken away from them, and then they will fast on that day. ...'[7]

> John the Baptist has come eating no bread and drinking no wine, and you say, 'He has a demon'; the Son of Man has come eating and drinking, and you say, 'Look, a glutton and a drunkard, a friend of tax-collectors and sinners!'[8]

And a second parting of the ways appears to have occurred over conditionality. John demanded repentance, but Jesus welcomed 'sinners' into the Kingdom of God without asking them to repent.

> And as he sat at dinner in Levi's house, many tax-collectors and sinners were also sitting with Jesus and his disciples – for there were many who followed him. When the scribes of the Pharisees saw that he was eating with sinners and tax-collectors, they said to his disciples, 'Why does he eat with tax-collectors and sinners?' When Jesus heard this, he said to them, 'Those who are well have no need of a physician, but

those who are sick; I have come to call not the righteous but sinners.'[9]

The most likely explanation for Jesus' diversity of approach is that as a disciple of John he believed that repentance and amendment of life were required before God's forgiveness could be received, but that he came to see that God's love was unconditional, that sinners were welcomed into the Kingdom of God without repentance being required, and that forgiveness was unconditional.[10] We might find it difficult to believe that forgiveness can be unconditional – but that is what Jesus appears to have come to believe.

It is on the basis of grace, of gift, of the centrality of forgiveness to the Christian Gospel, that Christians have campaigned for the forgiveness of debt.[11] Forgiveness is equally relevant to our benefits system. Conditional benefits are what we might call 'John the Baptist' benefits. They are conditional. Either we have to have paid in contributions in order to receive them, or we have to prove that we are looking for work, or we have to prove that we are not living with someone with earned income, or we have to give evidence of our income and savings … . Unconditional benefits are 'mature Jesus' benefits. There are no conditions. We are included, just as Jesus included unrepentant sinners in the Kingdom of God. There is nothing that we would be able to do that would exclude us from receiving our Citizen's Basic Incomes.[12] Quite simply, we are forgiven. We can decide not to work, we can decide to move in with someone, we can decide to start a small business, we can decide to spend more time caring for an elderly parent, we can spend our time surfing at the seaside, or we can care for a nature reserve. It won't matter what it is, and whether whatever it is is socially approved or disapproved.[13]

As the man whom Jesus forgave discovered, forgiveness resulted in his healing – which would no doubt have resulted in him making rather more of a contribution to life around him than he had been able to make before. Similarly, an unconditional Citizen's Basic Income will be an invitation to contribute, to work, to care, and to forgive. The bidirectional reciprocity will occur: not as a condition, but as a consequence.

And so the 'early Jesus' and the 'mature Jesus' attitudes to conditionality and to forgiveness will come together. Everyone's Citizen's Basic Income will be experienced as a release from conditionality; and everyone's Citizen's Basic Income will release them into new attitudes and new lifestyles. To experience unconditional forgiveness can generate unconditional forgiveness.

But as the master who forgave his servant a huge debt discovered, the process is far from automatic. We can understand the master's anger and his actions when his forgiveness did not find an echo in the servant's forgiveness of a fellow servant. We too might express anger if for some people their Citizen's Basic Incomes enabled them to spend more time watching day-time television. Our reaction would be understandable. But their Citizen's Basic Income would keep on arriving. Nothing would stop it; and we would find that Citizen's Basic Income and its recipients were nearer to the Kingdom of God than we could ever have imagined.

Citizen's Basic Income would ensure that workers would be paid for their work

The scripture says, 'You shall not muzzle an ox while it is treading out the grain', and, 'The labourer deserves to be paid.'
(1 Timothy 5:18)

'The labourer deserves to be paid' was probably a proverb. It is not found in the Old Testament in quite those terms, although a passage from the Book of Deuteronomy might lie behind it:

> You shall not withhold the wages of poor and needy labourers, whether other Israelites or aliens who reside in your land in one of your towns. You shall pay them their wages daily before sunset, because they are poor and their livelihood depends on them; otherwise they might cry to the Lord against you, and you would incur guilt.[1]

Jesus had used the proverb when sending his disciples out to preach:

> Remain in the same house, eating and drinking whatever they provide, for the labourer deserves to be paid. Do not move about from house to house.[2]

'You shall not muzzle an ox while it is treading out the grain' is found in precisely those terms in the Book of Deuteronomy,[3] and Paul used it to suggest that those who give their time and energy to preaching and teaching should be supported financially:

> For it is written in the law of Moses, 'You shall not muzzle an ox while it is treading out the grain.' Is it for oxen that God is concerned?[4]

– although in the Corinthian correspondence he is clear that he had never availed himself of that right, but had remained self-sufficient, presumably by making tents, which was his trade.

The passage from Deuteronomy is specific: a poor labourer should be paid at the end of the working day. They have earned their money, and it should be paid in full. As the Letter of James says to the rich:

> The wages of the labourers who mowed your fields, which you kept back by fraud, cry out, and the cries of the harvesters have reached the ears of the Lord of hosts.[5]

Such passages apply directly to the continuing scourge of wage theft (employers deducting till shortages from wages, and charging employees for uniforms, rather than the business paying for them): but they also apply to a problem that affects far more people: the scale of government deductions from additional earnings.

In the UK, a family receiving Housing Benefit, Council Tax Support, Working Tax Credits, and Child Tax Credits, and with the main breadwinner earning enough to be paying Income Tax and National Insurance Contributions, can find that each extra £1 that they earn will benefit the family's net income by just 4p.[6] This is because Income Tax and National Insurance Contributions will be deducted from each additional £1 earned, and the additional earnings will cause means-tested benefits (in this case, Working Tax Credits, Child Tax Credits, Housing Benefit, and Council Tax Support) to be reduced. The Department for Work and Pensions used to publish tables and graphs to illustrate the effects of benefits withdrawal on additional earnings across a wide range of earnings and for a variety of household types. The last year in which the tables were published in print was 2004; the tables then survived for five years on the internet, and in 2009 publication ceased entirely. It is quite true that if the Department for Work and Pensions succeeds in implementing Universal Credit, then the total withdrawal rate will drop to 76 per cent, but this still leaves the worker with only 24p of each additional £1 earned: and because the tables are no longer published, we will find it difficult to work out exactly what different household types' marginal deduction rates are likely to be.

No one is saying that governments should not be able to extract resources so that they can pay for public services. In the UK, a health service free at the point of use is a priceless asset that costs money; free education is essential to both our society and our economy; defense, the police, the judiciary, transport systems, communications infrastructure, and much else, are all essential to our life together. But there is something amiss when the wealthiest in the UK pay to the government 47p of every extra £1 that they earn, whereas the government benefits by 96p for every extra £1 earned by the lowest earners. The wealthiest mounted a vigorous campaign against a 50 per cent top rate of Income Tax, claiming that it would reduce incentives and drive skilled people abroad. They won. The fact that the lowest earners can be paying 12 per cent of additional earnings in National Insurance Contributions (whereas the wealthiest pay only 2 per cent), that the lowest earners might be paying 20 per cent in Income Tax on additional earnings if their earnings are already over the Income Tax Personal Allowance, and that benefits withdrawal can take the total withdrawal rate to 96 per cent, never becomes the subject of public comment, let alone of a campaign.

At the very least, the poor should benefit from additional earnings to the same extent as the wealthy, and preferably to a greater extent: which suggests that the total withdrawal rate inflicted on the poor should be no more than 47 per cent. An alternative approach would be to make National Insurance Contributions less regressive by ensuring that they were paid at 12 per cent on all earned income, which would mean that the total withdrawal rate on earnings suffered by the wealthy would be 57 per cent. We could then ensure that the withdrawal rate suffered by the lowest earners fell below that.

None of this could be achieved with a benefits system still based on means-tested benefits. To reduce the withdrawal rate of means-tested benefits below 15 per cent (47 per cent − 32 per cent), or below 25 per cent (57 per cent − 32 per cent) would mean that most low earning families would have to be earning staggering amounts of money before they would be free of means-tested benefits. This reveals one of the real difficulties with means-tested benefits. A steep taper − that is, rapid withdrawal of benefits as earnings rise − gets families off means-tested benefits reasonably quickly, but at the cost of huge withdrawal rates while that happens. A shallow taper − that is, slower withdrawal of benefits as earnings rise − results in lower withdrawal rates, but at the cost of the family never escaping from means-tested benefits. Only the abolition of means-tested benefits will solve the problem.

The main virtue of a Citizen's Basic Income is that it would never be withdrawn, and so would never contribute to marginal deduction rates: that is, to the total withdrawal rates on additional earnings. A Citizen's Basic Income scheme that was able to replace all means-tested benefits with an unconditional income for every individual would therefore solve the problem. The problem is that any conceivably affordable Citizen's Basic Income scheme would not be able to do that. As Appendix 1 shows, a Citizen's Basic Income that was paid for by abolishing the Income Tax Personal Allowance and most means-tested benefits would create losers among low income households, and so would not be feasible. The reason for the problem is that a household's Citizen's Basic Incomes would replace the value of their personal allowances, but could not at the same time replace all of their means-tested benefits − in this case, their Working Tax Credits and Child Tax Credits. The answer (in scheme B in Appendix 1) is to abolish the Income Tax Personal Allowance, use the savings to pay for a Citizen's Basic

Income, leave the means-tested benefits in place, and reduce every household's means-tested benefits by taking into account their Citizen's Basic Incomes in the same was as other income is taken into account when means-tested benefits are calculated. As the reader will see, this approach would reduce to almost zero the rate of losses that low income households would experience at the point of implementation, and it would also take large numbers of households off means-tested benefits or bring them within striking distance of taking themselves off them. So even though the means-tested structure would remain in place, for many households currently on means-tested benefits the system would no longer exist in practice. (An additional advantage offered by scheme B is that it would be extremely simple to implement, and could be implemented almost overnight. This could prove to be a significant advantage if the UK Government decides that Universal Credit is not fit for purpose – which it isn't.)

I first encountered the problem of high marginal deduction rates as a theoretical issue when I was administering means-tested benefits in Brixton between 1976 and 1978. Following ordination in the Church of England's ministry, and a curacy at the Elephant and Castle, also in South London, I became an industrial chaplain. One of my tasks was to be chaplain to the thousands of workers at St Thomas's Hospital. That was where I really came to understand the problem of high marginal deduction rates. A carpenter was pleased to have been promoted to foreman – and then wished that he had not been. His wages had risen, but the effects of additional Income Tax and National Insurance Contributions, and of the loss of Family Income Supplement (as the in-work means-tested benefit was then called), meant that he was no better off. He was not being rewarded for taking on considerable additional responsibility. The labourer was not being paid: the ox was being muzzled.

But perhaps 'the labourer deserves to be paid'[7] needs to be taken in another sense, too. In Jesus' parable of the vineyard workers,[8] all of the workers were paid the same, regardless of how many hours they put in. When the disciples arrived in a village to preach and heal, there is no sense that they were being paid a wage for the work that they were doing. Instead, they were being supported financially so that they could do the work that needed doing. They were receiving a temporary Citizen's Basic Income, which was enabling them to heal the sick and to preach the nearness and coming of the Kingdom of God. No doubt the villagers would have ceased to support them if no preaching or healing had materialised, but it is still true that while they were in the village they were fed so that they could do the work that needed doing, rather than being paid for the work that they had done. In many Churches, stipends paid to the Church's clergy are of a similar character. There might be mutual accountability between the Church's minister and a variety of stakeholders (the bishop, parish officers, congregational members, and so on), but there is no line management. The minister is expected to fulfil a variety of functions, but there is no sense in which they are being paid for a certain number of hours of work, or for meeting a variety of targets, or for performing specific tasks. They are being paid so that they can do the wide variety of work that their community and their congregation need them to be doing.

This is the structure of a Citizen's Basic Income. It provides for our needs – or at least for some of them – so that we can be free to do the work that needs doing: be that caring work, voluntary work in the community, creative work for which we shall be paid little or nothing, remunerative self-employment, or paid work for an employer. The Citizen's Basic Income provides opportunity. So yes, the labourer should be paid: not just because they have done some work, but also because they need to be supported financially so that they can do some work.

Citizen's Basic Income would be the basis of a covenant

I will establish my covenant between me and you, and your offspring after you throughout their generations, for an everlasting covenant, to be God to you and to your offspring after you.

(Genesis 17:7)

The first recorded covenant made by Israel's God was the one with Noah: to rescue him from the Flood, and to provide him with descendants;[1] and then, following the Flood, God established a covenant with the whole human race.[2] The passage quoted above records the covenant that God made with Abraham; the covenant was then renewed and further formalised with Moses; and, from then on, the Old Testament records Israel's frequent breaking of the covenant, God's reminders of them to keep it, and, crucially, God's constant faithfulness to the covenant that he had made.

> Because the Lord your God is a merciful God, he will neither abandon you nor destroy you; he will not forget the covenant with your ancestors that he swore to them.[3]

God has never abandoned Israel: a conviction to which Paul had to return following his conversion to Christ and his initial belief that the original covenant had been replaced.[4] God had made a covenant, and the covenant remained in force. The covenant enshrined a promise, and the promise would be kept.

Jeremiah had promised a 'new covenant',[5] and at his last meal with his disciples before his crucifixion Jesus established the expected new covenant:[6] a covenant accompanied by a vow that he would not again 'drink of the fruit of the vine until the kingdom of God comes',[7] and a covenant understood by early Christians to mean 'that those who are called may receive the promised eternal inheritance'.[8]

These three covenants – with the human race, with Israel, and with the Church – are all of the same character: they are all firm promises of commitment; and, most importantly, they are *unconditional* promises of commitment. At the same time, they invite a response. If the response fails to materialise, then the human race, Israel, or the Church, has broken the covenant: but the covenant remains in force, God remains committed to it, and the promise represented by the covenant will still be kept.

Very different from a covenant is a contract.[9] If two parties make a contract, and one party fails to fulfil their side of the contract, then the contract is broken, and that is the end of the contract – unless both parties agree to renew it. In most countries, contracts are enforceable: they have to be, or the economy would grind to a halt. If a parts manufacturer agrees to make a quantity of parts for a car manufacturer for a particular price, and the parts manufacturer does not make them, then the car manufacturer will not be able to build the cars that they had intended to build. They will suffer a financial loss, and ought to be able to extract compensation from the parts manufacturer. If the car manufacturer does not pay the parts manufacturer for parts delivered, then the parts manufacturer will suffer a financial loss, and ought to be able to extract the unpaid debt from the car manufacturer. A contract requires both sides to keep the bargain that they have made. A contract is different from a covenant. With a contract, both sides are in the same position, agreeing a set of terms that both parties must keep if the contract is to remain in force. With a covenant, a lead player makes a covenant. A response is required, and if the expected response does not transpire, then the covenant is broken, but it has not come to an end. The commitment made by the lead party remains in force, and the promise will still be kept.

To take an example that is sometimes described in terms of a covenant, and sometimes in terms of a contract: In marriage, both parties make firm promises. If one party breaks their promise (for instance, the promise of faithfulness), then, if the other party regards marriage as a contract, they can regard the other party's breaking of their promise as the signal that the marriage is at an end. However, if they regard marriage as a covenant, then the other party breaking their promise means that they have broken the covenant, but the covenant is not at an end. The promise remains in force: indeed, the promises made by both parties remain in force. Human promises are not divine promises, and human covenants are not divine covenants, so in practice a constant breaking of a human covenant is likely to bring it to an end: but that is not the case with the archetypal covenants that characterise God's relationships with the human race, with Israel, and with the Church. These are covenants that remain in force however many times we break them.

Means-tested and contributory benefits systems are usually constituted by contracts. If someone makes the required number of financial contributions, whether to a dedicated fund or as an earnings tax, then the government or some other organisation will pay a contributory benefit, often for a defined period of time, if a relevant contingency applies: unemployment, illness, industrial injury, disability, widowhood, old age, or some other contingency. The government's promise to pay is entirely conditional on the claimant having paid the required contributions and having fulfilled the required contingency condition. A means-tested benefit is paid when some relevant contingency applies: unemployment, illness, old age. An additional contingency also applies: an income too low to live on. There will generally be conditions attached: an obligation on the unemployed to look for employment, often in prescribed ways; an obligation on people who are ill to obtain a certificate from a doctor, or to attend a medical examination; an obligation on people with disabilities to attend an assessment of their ability to earn a living … . Evidence of these conditions having been met will be required, along with evidence of income, spouse's or partner's income, savings, household structure, number of children, and so on. If any of the conditions are not met then the claimant has broken the contract and benefits will cease or will be reduced.

Very different is an unconditional benefit, such as the UK's Child Benefit, the UK's National Health Service, or a Citizen's Basic Income. Unconditional benefits are founded on covenants. The government, on behalf of society as a whole, promises to pay: and payment will continue to be made. A response is often expected. Child Benefit is paid to enable parents to care for their children, but if parents are not the best of parents, then the Child Benefit will continue to be paid – unless of course a Social Service department decides that for the child's good they need to be removed from their parents, in which case the Child Benefit will be paid to any new home to which the child is moved. The National Health Service continues to be available to citizens of the UK however much or however little we respond to its provision by taking care of our health. Occasionally suggestions are made that abuse of our own health – by smoking, by drinking too much, or by some other means – might result in healthcare being withdrawn. Such proposals are generally just rhetoric, largely because administering them in a coherent way would be impossible, but also because unconditional benefits such as the NHS are based on a covenant between society as a whole and every individual within it. The financial security that Child Benefit provides, and the healthcare security that the NHS delivers, are posited on the covenantal character of the benefit. It is the unconditional nature of the promise that means that it works: administratively, psychologically, and in terms of the economy. An unconditional benefit is the simplest, and therefore the cheapest, kind to administer; unconditional benefits provide a level of psychological security that no conditional benefit could ever provide; and, in a variety of ways, unconditional benefits are economically efficient.

Take the example of in-work benefits. If they are means-tested, then they rise if wages fall, so they function as a 'dynamic' subsidy to wages: that is, they enable employers to allow wages to fall in real terms, because they know that the government will fill the increasing gap between wages and households' subsistence needs. An unconditional benefit would function as a 'static' subsidy. It would not rise as wages fell, so no longer would employers be able to allow wages to fall in real terms and know that they were not affecting their workers' livelihoods. Workforce pressure, and if necessary government action (for instance, via a genuine National Living Wage), would maintain the value of wages.

To take another example: Conditional and means-tested benefits regulations generally prescribe parameters: for instance, the number of hours of employment below which benefits might be reduced if the worker does not find additional hours of employment. Such benefits have different effects at different wage levels: so, for instance, means-tested benefits might make it less likely that anyone would be employed for a particular number of hours, because the resultant net income would not be above the net income generated by a lower number of hours. All of this creates rigidities and inefficiencies in the employment market (which generates economic inefficiencies for companies), and rigidities in families' employment pattern choices (making it difficult for families to establish the kinds of employment patterns that might best suit their circumstances, and particularly their caring responsibilities). An unconditional income would not create or exacerbate any of these rigidities because it would operate in precisely the same way whatever the wage level, whatever the number of hours worked, whatever the number of hours offered, and so on. The employment market would be able to function as something very close to a classical market, enabling the employment patterns offered to match the employment patterns wanted by both workers and employers.

For all manner of practical reasons, the covenantal nature of unconditional benefits – the way in which they never stop, whatever response is offered or not offered – generates considerable advantages when compared with the contract nature of contributory and means-tested benefits. But for the Christian, the covenantal nature of unconditional benefits offers a particularly clear advantage: it takes God's covenantal relationship with the human race, with Israel, and with the Church, as the model for our benefits system. We can therefore see that there is a clear theological difference between unconditional benefits and every other kind. Unconditional benefits cohere with the way in which God relates to us, whereas no other kind does.

But what of the response that God's covenants expect? As Paul puts it in relation to God's reconciliation with us when he writes to the Church in Corinth:

> All this is from God, who reconciled us to himself through Christ, and has given us the ministry of reconciliation; that is, in Christ God was reconciling the world to himself, not counting their trespasses against them, and entrusting the message of reconciliation to us. So we are ambassadors for Christ, since God is making his appeal through us; we entreat you on behalf of Christ, be reconciled to God.[10]

God has done the reconciling, and now it is the Corinthian Christians' responsibility to be reconciled with God. A covenant might constitute an unconditional promise, but there is still a response expected.

A less theological way of putting this discussion is to suggest that reciprocity[11] is required.

The first draft of my book *101 Reasons for a Citizen's Income* contained well over 101 reasons for a Citizen's Basic Income. Some of the reasons had to be culled, and one of the culled reasons was 'reciprocity'. With hindsight, that was a mistake. For a lot of people, the idea of reciprocity is at the heart of the concept of a just society. The 'Blue Labour' movement within the Labour Party believes, probably correctly, that the majority of people who live in the UK wish to live in a nation characterised by reciprocity rather than in one in which either the market or the state are relied upon for the satisfaction of our needs. Ed Miliband caught this mood when he offered a politics of 'something for something', and suggested that Income-related Jobseekers' Allowance should be higher for individuals with more consistent National Insurance Contribution records. Frank Field MP catches the same mood when he asks for an income maintenance strategy based on a renewed and enhanced National Insurance system.[12]

The desire for reciprocity is understandable. Many of us like to feel that we are making a contribution; our human dignity can be dented if we cannot provide for ourselves and for our dependents and have to rely on others for support, and we are not very keen on other people free-riding if we are working hard to support ourselves and our families – and them. All of this is perfectly natural and comprehensible.

But that still leaves unanswered the question: What precisely constitutes reciprocity? At the heart of the idea is two-way traffic. If I do something for you and you then do something for me, then you have reciprocated; and if you do something for me and I then do something for you, then I have reciprocated. The idea of reciprocity does not privilege an order of events: it simply requires that resources of some kind should travel in both directions in a relationship, and that the first transfer of resources should invite an answering transfer of some kind in the opposite direction.

It is therefore strange that in the income maintenance field 'reciprocity' usually does connote a particular order of events: that the individual should do something for society, and then society will do something for the individual. This is the assumption that lies behind the idea that the National Insurance system provides the best model for an income maintenance system characterised by reciprocity, and behind the objection that if everyone were to be given an unconditional income then no one would do the work that society needs to have done.[13] These are unwarranted assumptions. Society doing something for the individual, and then the individual doing something for society, would be just as reciprocal. Society providing each individual with a Citizen's Basic Income would reduce many people's marginal deduction rates, and so would make it more likely that they would seek additional earnings, learn new skills, start new businesses, give more time to their communities, come off means-tested benefits (thus saving administrative costs), and form permanent relationships: and because their earnings would be likely to be higher, they would be better able to lift their families out of poverty and at the same time pay more Income Tax. Reciprocity will have taken place.

Reciprocity characterises both contracts and covenants, but in different ways. In a covenant, the lead player promises, and the other party is invited to reciprocate. Lack of reciprocation does not negate the original promise. In a contract, reciprocation is required, and if it does not materialise then the contract is at an end – or reciprocation has to be enforced. Unconditional benefits such as Citizen's Basic Income constitute a firm commitment on the part of society, and then expect individuals to reciprocate, and provide them with the best possible context in which to do so. Conditional benefits require that recipients first of all fulfil some kind of condition, and then the state reciprocates with a payment. The reciprocation is in entirely different directions: but both generate a reciprocal relationship. It is not that conditional benefits cohere with our requirement for reciprocation and unconditional benefits do not. The theological difference is that the order of reciprocation that relates to unconditional benefits mirrors the reciprocation invited by God's covenants with the human race, with Israel, and with the Church, whereas the reciprocation that relates to conditional benefits does not. God's covenant with Noah requires a response from every human being; God's covenant with Israel requires faithfulness to the Law, and particularly to the requirement to worship God alone;[14] and the new covenant established by Jesus is accompanied by a variety of commands: to follow Jesus, to 'love one another', to make disciples and baptise them, and to share bread and wine 'in remembrance of him'.[15] Similarly, the gift of a Citizen's Basic Income would invite a response in terms of participation in the life of society: through employment, self-employment, caring work, creative activity, and voluntary work in the community. And just as the promise offered by God's covenants with the human race, with Israel, and with the

Church, makes possible the reciprocity invited, so a Citizen's Basic Income would make more possible the reciprocity required than means-tested or contributory benefits could ever do. A Citizen's Basic Income would not disincentivise employment, part-time employment, or self-employment, in the ways in which means-tested benefits disincentivise them; the employment patterns that it would make possible would make caring and voluntary activity more possible; and for those willing to live on very little, the opportunities for creative activity – which of course often results in financially beneficial activity – would be significantly enhanced.

The nature of the Christian covenant could not be put better than in the letter to the Ephesians:

> For by grace you have been saved through faith, and this is not your own doing; it is the gift of God — not the result of works, so that no one may boast. For we are what he has made us, created in Christ Jesus for good works, which God prepared beforehand to be our way of life.[16]

The order is crucial. First comes God's free and generous gift of salvation; and then our answering response: 'good works, which God prepared beforehand to be our way of life'. This is the Christian version of reciprocity, and it is the kind exemplified by Citizen's Basic Income.

Citizen's Basic Income would inspire us to be co-creators

Then God said, 'Let us make humankind in our image, according to our likeness; and let them have dominion over the fish of the sea, and over the birds of the air, and over the cattle, and over all the wild animals of the earth, and over every creeping thing that creeps upon the earth.' So God created humankind in his image,
in the image of God he created them;
male and female he created them.
God blessed them, and God said to them, 'Be fruitful and multiply, and fill the earth and subdue it; and have dominion over the fish of the sea and over the birds of the air and over every living thing that moves upon the earth.'

(Genesis 1:26–28)

This is not an easy passage. The mastery implied by the words 'subdue' and 'dominion' does not appear to imply the kind of careful stewardship that the health of the planet and its inhabitants requires, and it might be taken to imply the opposite. However, the statement that we are created in God's 'image' immediately precedes the command to 'be fruitful and multiply … subdue … have dominion:' so the fruitfulness, mastery, and dominion, are to be God's kind of fruitfulness, mastery, and dominion.

> The Lord God took the man and put him in the garden of
> Eden to till it and keep it.[1]

This is an invitation to join God in the work of creation, and the
fact that 'God saw that [the creation] was good'.[2] suggests that our
creative activity must also be directed towards a creation that is
good. So our fruitfulness, mastery, and dominion, are to be directed
towards God's kind of good creation, and the creation narratives
constitute an invitation to create in the way in which God creates,
for we are made in God's image.

However, the life of hard labour described in a further passage:

> By the sweat of your face
> you shall eat bread
> until you return to the ground,
> for out of it you were taken;
> you are dust,
> and to dust you shall return.[3]

looks very like the kind of exploitation that so many workers
experience today. The context is Adam and Eve eating the fruit of
the tree of the knowledge of good and evil, after which God says:
'See, the man has become like one of us, knowing good and evil':
and so that Adam and Eve could not eat the fruit of the tree of
life, they were banished from the Garden of Eden. 'By the sweat
of your face you shall eat bread until you return to the ground'
is a statement of fact. Agriculture was hard work, as it still is for a
large proportion of the world's population. But that is not all that
there is to be said about work. One of God's gifts is the skill to
create beautiful things, such as the tabernacle – the tent temple –
that God commanded Moses to build while Israel was wandering
in the wilderness:

> He has filled [the workers] with skill to do every kind of work
> done by an artisan or by a designer or by an embroiderer

in blue, purple, and crimson yarns, and in fine linen, or by a weaver – by any sort of artisan or skilled designer.[4]

God is a skilful creator, and we, who are made in God's image, receive as a gift of God's Spirit the skills that enable us to create skilfully:

> Do not say to yourself, 'My power and the might of my own hand have gained me this wealth.' But remember the Lord your God, for it is he who gives you power to get wealth, … .[5]

It is not that God is a creator and we are not creators. It will be hard work, yes: but at God's invitation, and through God's resourcing, we shall be co-creators, and the hard work will mirror the hard work that God does in creation. A covenant is involved: God has given us strength and skill; and the response required is hard creative work.

So why does one of Paul's letters contain a punitive attitude that looks rather like the sanctions regimes attached to so many modern 'labour market activation' strategies?

> For even when we were with you, we gave you this command: Anyone unwilling to work should not eat. For we hear that some of you are living in idleness, mere busybodies, not doing any work. Now such persons we command and exhort in the Lord Jesus Christ to do their work quietly and to earn their own living. Brothers and sisters, do not be weary in doing what is right.[6]

Paul's letters to the Church in Thessalonica are probably his earliest letters, and their context is an intense expectation that Jesus would soon return to establish his Kingdom. (The expectation that Jesus would come again in the foreseeable future seems to have evaporated by the time Paul wrote what was probably his last letter, the letter to the Romans.) This early Christian context makes sense of the earliest Christians selling their possessions and distributing the proceeds 'to all, as any had need'.[7] Christians who expected Jesus to return tomorrow, or perhaps even today, might have found it difficult to concentrate on caring for assets or working for a living. The sale of assets, and giving the proceeds to the poor, might have seemed both appropriate in the context, and a fulfilment of Jesus' command to the rich young ruler, who came to ask what he should do to gain eternal life. Jesus' answer was: 'Go, sell what you own, and give the money to the poor, and you will have treasure in heaven; then come, follow me.'[8]

Paul was firmly committed to the conviction that Jesus would return to establish his kingdom,[9] but he was also concerned for the ongoing life of the congregations that he had founded. Those congregations might be short-lived if Jesus were to return soon, but if his return might be delayed then they would need to sustain themselves in the longer term. It was therefore imperative that Church members should continue to work for a living. In the absence of a modern welfare state, the only way for a Church to continue to care for the poor – both its own poor members, and others too – was for its members to continue to earn money. The passage is not a justification for onerous benefits sanctions: it is an encouragement to all of us to do some creative and productive work during the interval between Christ's first and second comings, so that we might be able to provide the resources that we shall need if we are to care for the poor. As the Letter to the Ephesians puts it:

> thieves must give up stealing; rather let them labour and work honestly with their own hands, so as to have something to share with the needy.[10]

As we have already seen, grace is at the heart of the Christian tradition: but grace is not the tradition's only component, for the grace of God always comes as an invitation to respond, to be gracious ourselves in response to the grace of God. We speak of a gracious creator,[11] but we too are to be creators: co-creators. We create wealth just as much as wealth is given as a gift.

One particularly attractive characteristic of a Citizen's Basic Income is that it reflects the centrality of grace, and at the same time is an invitation to be creative, to co-create. It is an invitation to receive, and then to contribute with paid and unpaid work. Paid work would always be more lucrative in the context of a Citizen's Basic Income than it is in the context of means-tested benefits; and a Citizen's Basic Income would also give to people more freedom to create the packages of paid and unpaid work that would best suit their creative skills.

The point is the same from either a religious or a secular perspective. From a religious perspective, the created order is a gift of God, and we are invited to participate in God's creative activity. From a secular point of view, the universe, our solar system, and our planet, constitute a 'given' that invites our co-operation. Either way, the point is valid: wealth is both given and earned. The problem with our present income maintenance system is that too often it divides people into those who earn sufficient to keep themselves off means-tested benefits, and those who receive a grudging handout, and are largely prevented from improving their financial position by the way in which benefits are withdrawn as earned income rises. This means that neither group is expressing the truth as far as wealth-creation is concerned: that is, that wealth is both given and earned. With a Citizen's Basic Income everyone would receive an unconditional income, and everyone would have an opportunity to contribute, and would not be discouraged from doing so to the extent that many people are now. Everyone would be a recipient, and everyone would be a contributor in one way or another: so everyone would experience wealth as both given and earned, and would experience themselves as co-creators of that wealth.

But if we simply gave everyone some money, would the necessary work still get done? The sun's energy might be free, but in order to capture it we need to build solar panels; to produce food we need to sow seed, look after the crop, harvest it, transport it, and sell it; and to provide drinkable water we need to capture the water, process it, and provide the infrastructure required to get it into people's homes. All of this requires work, and we would need to be sure that it would get done: so we naturally ask the question: 'How can we make people work?' However, we could rephrase the question: 'How can we distribute the proceeds of production in such a way that people are most likely to do the work required to provide the goods and services that society needs?' If we ask the question 'How can we make people work?' then we might answer: 'By paying them if they work', or 'Only pay them benefits if they look for work'. If we ask the second question, then the answer is different: 'If we give to everyone an unconditional income, and we pay people to work, then we shall encourage them to put in the required effort'. Means-tested benefits are withdrawn as earned income rises, so additional earned income can result in very little additional disposable income. A payment that is not withdrawn does not have this effect, and so increases employment incentives.[12] A further effect of a Citizen's Basic Income is that it would provide a level of financial security that would enable individuals and households to take risks: to seek new skills, to start a new business, or to look for a new job.[13]

The anxiety that if we simply gave everybody some money then they would not work is understandable. The fact that people would be more likely to work if they were given Citizen's Basic Incomes than if they remained on means-tested benefits (including such in-work benefits as Working Tax Credits and Universal Credit) suggests that we have no reason not to provide everybody with a Citizen's Basic Income.

One of the serious dislocations caused by our current income maintenance system is the way in which it privileges work for pay over work without payment, and because unpaid labour in the home is more often undertaken by women than it is by men, the result is that our income maintenance system tends to privilege 'men's work' over 'women's work'. The UK's means-tested benefits system might require someone receiving benefits and undertaking caring work, voluntary activity, or a training course, to abandon their caring, their training, or their voluntary activity in order to seek or accept employment. The training might have led to more creative work which would have been of benefit to them, to society, and to the economy; their caring – of neighbours or family members – might be a substantial service to the community; and their voluntary labour might have led to more creative outcomes than the paid work that they were being forced to accept: but no matter – paid employment now, today, must be given priority. Earning a living is certainly important – and a Citizen's Basic Income, by reducing marginal deduction rates, would always make earning a living more efficient than it is now for any household currently on means-tested benefits (including in-work benefits): but caring, training, and voluntary activity, can be equally important. A Citizen's Basic Income might enable someone to live without employment and without means-tested benefits for a while in order to do some useful training, some inspired voluntary work, or some necessary caring; and a Citizen's Basic Income would also make it easier for people to create more diverse employment patterns that would continue to give them the time to undertake training and voluntary activity when they wanted to, either alongside paid employment, or interspersed with periods of paid employment. As Paul puts it in his letter to the Church in Rome:

> For as in one body we have many members, and not all the members have the same function, so we, who are many, are one body in Christ, and individually we are members one of another. We have gifts that differ according to the grace given to us.[14]

This is as true of our life in society as it is of the diversity of Christians in the Church: and the more opportunity everyone has to discover, develop and use their many gifts – for gifts are gifts – the more fruitful will be our co-creation.

Wealth is both given and earned. The keyboard on which I am typing this has been made from raw materials given in God's creation, and it has been manufactured using skills that God and other people have given to the manufacturers, or to the robots that manufacturers have made and that have then made the keyboard.

All wealth is given and earned. God's invitation to us to be co-creators is an invitation to participate in the earning of wealth: a diverse wealth, and not simply the sort generated by paid employment. So the individual using their God-given time, compassion, and skills, to care for a relative or friend, and the amateur artist who uses their God-given talent to create paintings for a local exhibition, are as much participants in the creation of wealth that is both given and earned as are the teacher who is paid for imparting a wealth of knowledge and the wind turbine engineer who uses their God-given energy and skill to create a turbine out of materials given in God's creation.

An important question relates to the engineer who uses God-given skills and God-given material to create a coal-fired power station that will contribute to global warming and climate change: or indeed to anyone engaged in activity that is destructive of God's creation and of human wellbeing. The way in which our economy is organised means that many people have little choice over their paid employment. Someone living in a town with a single large arms-manufacturer as the only employer will either have to work for that company or they will have to move. The social and financial disruption that moving can cause a family might mean that working for the arms manufacturer is the only viable option, however morally ambiguous such employment might be. In some cases a Citizen's Basic Income would offer some additional options, such as the ability to start a co-operative enterprise that employed existing skills for more socially useful purposes:[15] but that might not be a viable option for everyone in this situation. A Citizen's Basic Income would enable people more easily to refuse jobs that were of poor quality, or that destroyed wealth rather than creating it, and the outcome would be better jobs, and thus work that more clearly contributed to our personhood, and that recognised that work is a means and not an end. The end that is served by work is human flourishing, and a Citizen's Basic Income would make that a lot clearer and a lot more possible.[16]

A Citizen's Basic Income would recognise that all wealth is both given and earned, and that not all wealth is created by paid employment. Money is the way in which our society normally ascribes value, and it is the way in which we recognise that wealth has been created. The salary that arrives at the end of each month, or the self-employed worker's rising bank balance, is experienced as a statement that wealth has been created. Someone who is not paid to care for a relative, to tend a nature reserve, or to run a youth club, does not have the wealth that they have created recognised in the same way. Means-tested benefits certainly do not function as a sign of such recognition. If the carer or volunteer begins to earn an income, then their means-tested benefits are removed, even if the caring or voluntary work continues. A Citizen's Basic Income would function entirely differently. It would keep on coming – and it would keep on coming for everyone – and it might therefore function as a monetary recognition of the contribution that everyone is making to society, one way or another.

True, there are some people about whom we might wish to say that they were not creating wealth of any kind; and there are some who actively destroy the wealth that other people create. For some of these individuals, receipt of a Citizen's Basic Income would generate a sense of social inclusion that might lead to a more participative and creative attitude to life. It would be interesting to find out how many people would be affected in this way. What is not a problem is the possibility that some people would live very cheaply on their Citizen's Basic Income and spend their days on a surfboard, or undertaking some other activity that might look to everyone else like self-indulgence. First of all, the lower marginal deduction rates that a Citizen's Basic Income would deliver, in comparison to those experienced with means-tested benefits, would encourage the surfer to undertake at least a small amount of paid employment; secondly, they might also use their time to care for or educate other members of the surfing community; and thirdly, beautiful surfing is as much a kind of wealth as is an art installation. A Citizen's Basic Income would not discriminate between different kinds of wealth, and nor would it require different kinds of wealth to be measured and then compared. A Citizen's Basic Income would continue to be paid, whatever kinds of wealth the individual was creating with their God-given skills, and with their own time and energy. Wealth is always earned and given. A Citizen's Basic Income would recognise that, and would encourage a great deal of wealth creation of many different kinds.

A significant problem related to means-tested benefits is the social stigma attached to them. The arduous application process, the sanctions, the constant reporting of circumstances, the frequent requests for evidence, the enquiries into the intimate details of relationships, and the calculation errors, add up to a seriously disempowering experience. It is easy to say that attitudes towards the unemployed need to change, or that we need a new life ethic to replace the work ethic that drives both overwork and the stigmatisation of unemployment, but only a changed system will deliver the required change in attitude. We shall only be able to value each individual as a unique child of God, and as someone invited to co-create with God, if our social and economic structures value everyone equally as the recipient of a share in a wealth that is given, and as individuals invited to offer a variety of creative responses. A Citizen's Basic Income would contribute to the changed system that we need, and it would generate a large part of the attitude change required.

It is sometimes argued that the Government providing everyone with a job would be more effective than providing everyone with an income.[17] There are arguments both for and against a Government job guarantee. The Government creating a job for everyone who doesn't have one could provide participants with purposeful activity: but because the jobs would be artificially manufactured, there would always be the sense that the work wasn't necessary. Perhaps the more serious objections are that the experience of the Manpower Services Commission in the UK during the 1980s suggests that policing and supervising job guarantee schemes can be difficult and costly, and that manufactured jobs can displace employment market jobs, and can therefore make the employment market even less efficient than it is now. But we do not need to decide here whether job creation schemes are a good idea. What does need to be said here is that a job guarantee scheme and a

Citizen's Basic Income could function perfectly happily together. There is no need to choose between them.

As we have seen in the biblical passages that we have studied, work is a somewhat ambiguous issue. On the one hand, God gives the skills for highly creative work; and, on the other, work is experienced as an unfortunate necessity. We need an income maintenance system that would emphasise the first of those characteristics, and minimise the second. A Citizen's Basic Income would contribute to such a system. Anyone in full-time employment, and enabled by their Citizen's Basic Income to extract themselves from means-tested benefits, would no longer have their energy sapped by the social censure communicated by means-tested benefits regulations. The additional energy available for community and caring activity could be considerable. Also, with a Citizen's Basic Income, anyone not in employment would be more able to accept employment that would benefit their family's financial position. Work would become more of a personal response to God's creative activity and less of an unfortunate but necessary means of making sufficient money to live on.

11.

Citizen's Basic Income would understand both our original righteousness and our original corruption

Then God said, 'Let us make humankind in our image,
according to our likeness … .'
So God created humankind in his image,
in the image of God he created them;
male and female he created them.

… God saw everything that he had made, and indeed, it was
very good. And there was evening and there was morning, the
sixth day.

(Genesis 1:26–27, 31)

For I know my transgressions,
and my sin is ever before me.
Against you, you alone, have I sinned,
and done what is evil in your sight,
so that you are justified in your sentence
and blameless when you pass judgement.
Indeed, I was born guilty,
a sinner when my mother conceived me.

(Psalm 51:3–5)

The consensus of the Old Testament is that human beings were part of God's 'good' creation, but that there is now something inherently corrupt about us. The New Testament writers are of the same view. In his letter to the Romans, Paul wrote this:

> But now, irrespective of law, the righteousness of God has been disclosed, and is attested by the law and the prophets, the righteousness of God through faith in Jesus Christ for all who believe. For there is no distinction, since all have sinned and fall short of the glory of God; they are now justified by his grace as a gift, through the redemption that is in Christ Jesus.[1]

Any righteousness that we might possess has to be imputed by God rather than being a righteousness that we ourselves exercise. Or does it? Doesn't the passage suggest that we earn our righteousness through the faith that we exercise? The matter is not so simple, as there is a significant ambiguity in what Paul wrote. The translation offered, from the New Revised Standard Version, 'through faith in Jesus Christ', translates a plain genitive, with no preposition. It should probably be translated 'through faith of Jesus Christ', or 'through Jesus Christ's faith'. The New Revised Standard Version puts this alternative translation in a footnote. Most other translations also go for 'faith in Jesus Christ', even though the alternative is probably what Paul meant. I suppose that the translators believe that if we cannot manage our own righteousness then at least we can manage our own faith. Paul didn't think so. Even the faith on which our new imputed righteousness is based is not our own: it is Jesus' faith in God that is the source of both our faith and our righteousness. God's relationship with us is a pure gift. It is not something that we earn, by righteous deeds or by anything else.

But let us not lose the conviction contained in the first chapter of the book of Genesis: that God has made us in his image, that we are still created in the image of God, that God's creation is good, and that we are still part of that good creation. We are innately good as well as innately corrupt; we exhibit both a tendency to altruism and a tendency to evil.

So should we be optimistic about human nature, or should we be pessimistic? Should we believe that men and women are capable of creating utopia? Or should we be realistic, and believe that all that we can hope for is sufficient control of our evil tendencies to enable human society not to disintegrate entirely?

Let us begin with the 'original righteousness' that we find expressed in the passage from the book of Genesis. Human history is littered with examples of extreme altruism; and in our own families, friendships, and communities, genuine moral goodness can frequently be found. In the UK, blood for transfusions is collected from willing volunteers who will never know to whom they have donated their blood. No payment is made. This is a 'gift relationship', and one that Richard Titmuss suggests should form a model for social policy.[2] Genuine altruism here forms the basis for a gift: that is, an original righteousness makes possible an act of grace. The way in which Titmuss links the individual giving blood to the National Health Service giving blood to those who need it shows that altruism is both a personal and an institutional behaviour. This suggests that original righteousness and original sin can be institutional characteristics and not simply characteristics exhibited by individuals.

The causal relationship between original righteousness and altruism might be more complex than we might have thought. As Michael Sandel suggests on the basis of Titmuss's research, a market-driven society can erode altruism, and altruistic behaviour can create a society in which more of it takes place. Altruism creates a kind of social original righteousness that generates yet more altruism.[3]

Philip Wogaman has correctly pointed out that 'original righteousness' comes in two forms – the idea that as individuals we are good; and the idea that we are relational beings, and that goodness resides in our relationships with others. He calls these two perspectives 'integrity' and 'mutuality'.[4] As he suggests, they belong together: and this combination of the good individual in good relationships provides perhaps the best 'original righteousness' justification for Citizen's Basic Income. To give to every individual a

Citizen's Basic Income, without conditions, without sanctions, and without any questions being asked, is to assume the goodwill of the individual recipient: that they will use their Citizen's Basic Income as a springboard for the exercise of their righteousness, for the benefit of themselves and the world around them. To give Citizen's Basic Incomes to people understood as relational beings is to trust them to share both their Citizen's Basic Incomes and the beneficial effects of Citizen's Basic Incomes across their relationships; and to trust that the families and communities to which people belong will use their collective Citizen's Basic Incomes for the benefit of themselves and their communities. To take the example of the family: each individual's Citizen's Basic Income will enable them to make their own choices about type of employment, number of hours of employment, number of hours of caring work, number of hours of voluntary work, and so on: and a family's Citizen's Basic Incomes will enable the family's members to work together as they plan their employment, caring, and volunteering activities, so that those activities will serve the family's own needs and the needs of their community.

The Citizen's Basic Income debate attracts its fair share of utopians: those who believe that it is possible to build a just society, and that a Citizen's Basic Income is a necessary and feasible step towards this goal. Such participants are optimistic about human nature. They believe that we can plan, establish and maintain a Citizen's Basic Income scheme that would achieve all of the desired effects for individuals and society, and that none of the predicted ill-effects (such as greater apathy) would materialise. Then there are the realists, who believe that a Citizen's Basic Income scheme is one means of controlling some of the evil tendencies in our society, such as social fragmentation, the domination of women by men, the disincentive effects of the poverty and unemployment traps, the stigma related to means-tested benefits, and the consequential apathy. Both emphases are required.

The American statesman and theologian Reinhold Niebuhr is the last century's apostle of realism. His *Moral Man and Immoral Society*[5] said that when people with good intentions get together to carry out by good means a project with good ends, then the results will always be tainted with evil. 'The higher the aspirations rise the more do sinful pretensions accompany them.'[6] Niebuhr rightly saw that social conflict is inevitable, and that the use of force is essential in any society that hopes for a tolerable way of life. Approximations to ideals such as 'equality' and 'liberty' are all that will ever be possible. 'Let those who are revolted by ... ambiguities have the decency to retire to the monastery, where medieval perfectionists found their asylum.'[7] Thus strong trade unions are necessary brakes on the ability of large corporations to exploit workers; and only democratic governments can protect consumers and the environment from exploitation. Niebuhr was the theologian of the 'balance of power'. An optimistic assessment of human nature might be a necessary source of energy when it comes to challenging traditional forms of authority and social structure: but optimism, left to its own devices, will destroy both itself and its achievement. Optimism always needs to be balanced by realism about our individual and collective self-interest. By the end of his career as a theologian, political philosopher and statesman, Niebuhr believed the United States to have reached a situation wanted neither by realists nor by idealists, but that at least kept tolerable order: the politics of universal franchise and some well-organised trade unions between them controlling to some extent the worst abuses of excessive economic power.[8]

If the Citizen's Basic Income idea had come across Niebuhr's radar then I am sure that he would have treated it in the same way as he treated democracy. He would have regarded a Citizen's Basic Income as a possibility because of our idealism, and as a necessity because of our tendency to corruption. Our idealism tells us that if we provide individuals with an unconditional and nonwithdrawable income then they will want to contribute to society through paid and unpaid work. Our understanding of our tendency to corruption tells us that we will only commit ourselves to hard work in the service of society if we can increase our disposable income by doing so. A Citizen's Basic Income would contribute an original gift that would inspire responsibility, and it would enable us more easily to increase our disposable income through paid work because it would offer lower marginal deduction rates than means-tested benefits. A Citizen's Basic Income is precisely the kind of social policy that Niebuhr would have been looking for. With part of ourselves we want to give: but other parts of ourselves require incentives if we are to satisfy our own and others' needs through employment that might not be ideal or interesting.

A question that the realist might ask is this: What is the least bad form of government? The answer is 'democracy', because it recognises that power corrupts, and it enables a country's population to dismiss power-corrupted governments. The realist might ask a similar question of different benefits systems: Given that there will never be a tax and benefits system that satisfies everyone, or that responds adequately both to our original righteousness and to our original corruption, what would be the least bad option? The answer has to be a Citizen's Basic Income, because it recognises that incentives are important, and it provides the most effective way of turning additional earnings into additional net income. It also recognises that the street-level bureaucrats who manage the casework approach of means-tested systems will themselves be corrupted by the benefits system that they administer, and that both the system and the bureaucrats will mistreat claimants. The only answer is to abandon casework and establish a system that requires as little administration as possible. Again, the only answer is a Citizen's Basic Income.

Wogaman wonders whether a Citizen's Basic Income would cause people to disengage from democratic government.[9] The answer is no, it would not. First of all, because most Citizen's Basic Income schemes envisage the abolition of personal tax allowances, more people would be paying more income tax, and political engagement would therefore rise. Secondly, Citizen's Basic Income schemes often envisage linking receipt of a Citizen's Basic Income to being on the electoral register. The Citizen's Basic Income could therefore provide the most effective mechanism possible for ensuring that every individual was registered to vote. Democracy would be enhanced: so the system of government that recognises that we are both innately good and innately corrupt would benefit from the benefits system that would most effectively recognise both our original righteousness and our original corruption.

Both original righteousness and corruption are true of human nature, and a Citizen's Basic Income would cohere with both aspects: but there is still more to be said. Neither original righteousness, nor our corruption, nor a recognition of both, provides the most Christian reason for pursuing the debate on Citizen's Basic Income. The most Christian basis for doing that is the Kingdom of God, which Jesus has already lived, which has 'come near',[10] which God will complete, and of which there are already signs of its coming. We know some of the characteristics of the Kingdom of God through the life and teaching of Jesus: grace, justice, forgiveness, and love, would be at the top of the list. To reflect these and other characteristics of the Kingdom of God in our social institutions as well as in our personal lives is to live in God's Kingdom now, whatever else might be true of the original righteousness and corruption of ourselves or of anything else. As Sean Doherty puts it:

> If we want to see a more just economic order, we need to focus on the glorious hope of the Kingdom of God as a present as well as a future reality. ... God is advancing God's Kingdom, but we have a role to play within it. The notion that it is God who brings the Kingdom into history should not be misconstrued as implying that human action has no role to play, because human action can be taken up and used precisely by God.[11]

Citizen's Basic Income would recognise our mutual dependency

For just as the body is one and has many members, and all the members of the body, though many, are one body, so it is with Christ. For in the one Spirit we were all baptised into one body – Jews or Greeks, slaves or free – and we were all made to drink of one Spirit. Indeed, the body does not consist of one member but of many. ... If all were a single member, where would the body be? As it is, there are many members, yet one body. The eye cannot say to the hand, 'I have no need of you', nor again the head to the feet, 'I have no need of you.' ...
God has so arranged the body, giving the greater honour to the inferior member, that there may be no dissension within the body, but the members may have the same care for one another. If one member suffers, all suffer together with it; if one member is honoured, all rejoice together with it. Now you are the body of Christ and individually members of it.
(1 Corinthians 12:12–14, 19–21, 24–27)

In his first letter to the Church in Corinth Paul says something quite remarkable: that Christians *are* the risen Christ.[1] 'For just as the body is one and has many members ... so it is with Christ': and he then goes on to write about the Church and its many members as if it is entirely unproblematic that Christ and the Church are one and the same.[2] Paul's identification of Christ and the Church makes the way that the Church is constructed a theological matter, and not simply an organisational one (although it is that as well, of course[3]): and at the heart of the theological reality of the Church is a fundamental unity and interdependence between the Church's members, founded on each member's direct relationship with the body, which is Christ. One important consequence is that any organisational distinctions that we create within our Churches, by ordaining clergy, appointing moderators, or electing elders, are entirely secondary. Another is stated in the letters to the Corinthians and to the Galatians: that one member's suffering is every member's suffering, and that one member's burden is every member's burden.[4]

Our mutual dependence is a crucial doctrinal matter. We belong together in Christ, or we do not belong at all. We relate to God as mutually dependent members of Christ, and not as disconnected individuals. The earliest Christians gave very practical expression to this conviction by disposing of their possessions and sharing out the proceeds: a disposal of assets that was probably one of the reasons for the later poverty that motivated Paul to make a collection for the Church in Judea.[5]

When we come to ask about the characteristics of the relationships that we might expect to find in the Church, we might find Martin Buber's book *I and Thou* helpful.[6] Buber offers a vision of relationships between persons, a vision opposed to the tendency in our society to treat people as objects to whom we relate in an 'I–It' fashion. We are truly ourselves only in a web of relationships in which we change and mature one another, and in which the community is more than a simple sum of the characteristics of the people involved. Paul's vision of our mutual dependency in Christ, filled out by Buber's description of interpersonal relationships as 'I–Thou', has inspired many to work for a society characterised by equal membership and mutual dependency; and there is a long tradition of the solidarity of worshipping communities giving birth to political solidarities in trade unions and political parties.

There is little support for human rights in the Old and New Testaments,[7] but there is plenty of support for mutual dependence and for the mutual responsibility that that requires. The law that we find codified in the first five books of the Old Testament is a complex prescription for mutual responsibility in a society that included both the whole people of Israel and also resident aliens:

> Every third year you shall bring out the full tithe of your produce for that year, and store it within your towns; the Levites, because they have no allotment or inheritance with you, as well as the resident aliens, the orphans, and the widows in your towns, may come and eat their fill so that the Lord your God may bless you in all the work that you undertake.[8]

This is not simply a matter of one individual caring for another, as in Jesus' parable of the Good Samaritan.[9] What is envisaged is co-ordinated community provision. If Israel, Jesus' miracles, and the Church, are foretastes of the Kingdom of God, then that Kingdom will be characterised by both mutual dependence and mutual responsibility: and Christians will naturally wish to fashion our society so that it functions as a signpost towards that Kingdom. This will mean doing all that we can to create a society of mutually dependent members exercising mutual responsibility for each other. It is this kind of society that William Temple looked for when he described four Christian principles formulated at a conference on Christian Politics, Economics, and Citizenship, held in 1924: 'the sacredness of personality ... fellow-membership ... the duty of service ... the power of sacrifice'.[10] Whether we employ his term 'fellow-membership', the more secular 'fraternity', or the similarly secular but less masculine 'solidarity', we shall be seeking a society characterised by mutual dependence and nourished by mutual responsibility.

Such a vision struggles to be heard now in the West, either as an ideal at which to aim, or as a reality that we might experience. Our lives have become privatised because so many activities are now undertaken as individuals or as families, and far fewer as communities. Trade unions now offer services to individual members; we go on holiday as families rather than picking hops as communities; we watch videos or drink at home rather than going to the cinema or the pub; and we go to church as individuals seeking out the religion that we want in the supermarket of religions rather than going to the church or the chapel of the community in which we live. Performance-related pay divides one person from another. However, the best employers understand that when groups of people are responsible for tasks, then tasks get done more efficiently. We do not in fact naturally put our own interests first, whatever certain economists and politicians might think. We belong to one another, and deep down we know that the good of those among whom we live and work is our own good, and that to live selfishly does no one any good.

The beginning of the Christian Church saw a remarkable exercise in mutual responsibility:

> Now the whole group of those who believed were of one heart and soul, and no one claimed private ownership of any possessions, but everything they owned was held in common. … Awe came upon everyone, because many wonders and signs were being done by the apostles. All who believed were together and had all things in common; they would sell their possessions and goods and distribute the proceeds to all, as any had need. Day by day, as they spent much time together in the temple, they broke bread at home and ate their food with glad and generous hearts, praising God and having the goodwill of all the people. And day by day the Lord added to their number those who were being saved.[11]

The mutual responsibility exercised here went deeper than a provision for widows, resident aliens, or any other relatively deprived group. It might have been true that there was a conditionality attached – 'as any had need' – so that the distribution did not appear to be entirely on Jesus' feeding miracles, [12] in which there were no conditionalities: but the fact that 'no one claimed private ownership of any possessions, but everything they owned was held in common',[13] suggests first of all that not all of their assets were sold, and secondly that there was a significant level of equality.

With hindsight, the disposal of assets and the distribution of the proceeds 'to all'[14] might not have been such a brilliant idea: and in any case, the wholesale sale of assets and the distribution of the proceeds would not be a realistic proposition for most people living in a modern society: but we could at least take Jesus' feeding miracles as our model,[15] and represent the Kingdom of God by implementing as much unconditional and universal social provision as we can. In the UK, the National Health Service, Child Benefit, the Winter Fuel Allowance, and free education for every child up to the age of eighteen, are significant examples of provision that mirrors Jesus' feeding of the five thousand and the four thousand. An important achievement of the Liberal Democrats during the 2010–2015 Coalition Government was the provision of free school meals for every child in state schools up to the age of seven. Providing a meal to which everyone is invited constitutes a significant modern parable of the Kingdom of God.

All of this raises the question as to which social level is the most appropriate for the construction of mutual dependence and the exercise of mutual responsibility. We expect both within a family; a neighbourhood needs to be characterised by mutual dependence and is a natural context for the exercise of mutual responsibility; a region or a nation state needs to structure mutual responsibility if mutual dependence is to be a lived experience; and globally, mutual dependence and mutual responsibility between nations is becoming an urgent necessity, and in relation to climate change negotiations is becoming more of a reality. At which of these levels would a Citizen's Basic Income be most useful? To be realistic, apart from brief local pilot projects, Citizen's Basic Incomes are most likely to be implemented at the level of the nation state: but within such an implementation there would be clear benefits for families and neighbourhoods. Somewhat counterintuitively, individual Citizen's Basic Incomes would improve mutual responsibility within any family currently on means-tested benefits, because means-tested benefits are so likely to damage mutual responsibility. The fact that earned income reduces the household's benefits is a discouragement to earning an income or to earning additional income; and the fact that forming a permanent relationship can remove a lone parent's independent benefits income is no way to foster the kind of mutual responsibility that a relationship requires.

A Citizen's Basic Income would also enhance mutual responsibility within a neighbourhood, because people would be more able to choose the kinds of employment patterns that might facilitate caring and voluntary community responsibilities. At the level of a nation state's society, the fact that everyone would receive a Citizen's Basic Income, the fact that everyone earning an income would be contributing towards the cost of those Citizen's Basic Incomes, and the fact that everyone's Citizen's Basic Income would be an invitation to contribute to society in some way, would for the first time recognise in our tax and benefits system our mutual dependence and our mutual responsibility. A global Citizen's Basic Income might be some way off, but we ought not to discount the possibility. Pilot studies in Namibia and India have shown how effective a small Citizen's Basic Income can be at fighting poverty, at empowering individuals, and at facilitating democracy: so a global Citizen's Basic Income would tackle poverty globally, would encourage economic activity where it is most needed, could distribute the world's resources more equitably, would promote democracy, and would stem the flow of economic and other migrants. We might still be a few years away from Citizen's Basic Incomes at the level of the nation state, but that is no reason not to start discussions about a global Citizen's Basic Income now. We are quite capable of implementing one if we choose to do so. Perhaps a regional Citizen's Basic Income would be a useful first step. A Citizen's Basic Income for the European Union would facilitate the free market in labour, could obviate the need for regional adjustment funds, and would provide a useful lived experience of our fellow-membership of Europe. But in the meantime we need to concentrate on establishing a Citizen's Basic Income in each nation state. This is not to diminish our ambition. Such a single-nation Citizen's Basic Income would provide a model for other nations to follow, and once several nations had established Citizen's Basic Income schemes, existing Citizen's Basic Incomes would provide a model for regional or global Citizen's Basic Income schemes to follow.[16]

We all need autonomy: but the pendulum has swung too far in that direction. We need each other in order to be human, and to be mature as individuals in relationship. A Citizen's Basic Income at any level would tell us that we belong together because everyone would receive it, it would be paid for corporately, and it would contribute to a pendulum-swing in a social and community direction. Our interdependence would be embodied in our income structure, the wealth created by society would benefit everyone, everyone would be responsible for creating the diverse provision that society needs, and the Citizen's Basic Income would provide something like the ideal conditions for exercising the mutual responsibility that mutual dependence requires.

We need the pendulum to swing away from isolated individualism and towards the kind of society represented by William Temple's 'the sacredness of personality … fellow-membership … the duty of service … the power of sacrifice'.[17] Simon Duffy suggests that if Temple were writing today then he would see Citizen's Basic Income as a way to achieve that.[18]

13.

Citizen's Basic Income would facilitate a more just society

For the Lord your God is God of gods and Lord of lords, the great God, mighty and awesome, who is not partial and takes no bribe, who executes justice for the orphan and the widow, and who loves the strangers, providing them with food and clothing.

(Deuteronomy 10:17–18)

The Jewish Law commands the people of Israel: 'You shall not render an unjust judgement; you shall not be partial to the poor or defer to the great: with justice you shall judge your neighbour';[1] the prophet Jeremiah calls on them to 'act justly one with another, … do not oppress the alien, the orphan, and the widow, or shed innocent blood … ;[2] and in Isaiah, God says of his 'Servant': 'I have put my spirit upon him; he will bring forth justice to the nations. … he will faithfully bring forth justice. He will not grow faint or be crushed until he has established justice in the earth … .'[3] The prophet might have had a contemporary figure in mind, but Christians have always interpreted the passage as referring to Jesus.[4]

Jesus looked for justice:

> Woe to you, scribes and Pharisees, hypocrites! For you tithe mint, dill, and cummin, and have neglected the weightier matters of the law: justice and mercy and faith. It is these you ought to have practised without neglecting the others.[5]

The message is this: God's actions are characterised by justice, and ours should be as well. The content of the 'justice' intended is suggested by the passages themselves: justice means not being partial, not taking bribes, providing people with what they need, loving strangers, taking care of the most vulnerable, and making just judgements: presumably judgements characterised by provision for the poor and by ensuring that everyone receives equal treatment. In the passage from the New Testament we find Jesus calling on the religious establishment of his day to exercise justice; and in the parable of the unjust judge[6] (which ought really to be called the parable of the reluctantly just judge) Jesus tells a story that compares the justice that a judge delivers reluctantly to the true justice that God will vigorously administer. The judge should have known better. It is a widow who asks him for justice: precisely the kind of person for whom the passage from Deuteronomy demands justice; and as the passage from Leviticus suggests, the judge ought to have treated the widow in the same way as he would have treated someone wealthier and with a more secure social status.

In relation to the culture of his time, Jesus might have been as close to treating women in the same way as men as it was possible to get. Early on he chose twelve men to be his closest followers,[7] but he was soon accompanied by a matching group of female disciples:

> Soon afterwards he went on through cities and villages, proclaiming and bringing the good news of the kingdom of God. The twelve were with him, as well as some women who had been cured of evil spirits and infirmities: Mary, called Magdalene, from whom seven demons had gone out, and Joanna, the wife of Herod's steward Chuza, and Susanna, and many others, who provided for them out of their resources.[8]

It was some of these women who were present at Jesus' crucifixion:

> There were also women looking on from a distance; among them were Mary Magdalene, and Mary the mother of James

the younger and of Joses, and Salome. These used to follow him and provided for him when he was in Galilee; and there were many other women who had come up with him to Jerusalem.[9]

It was some of these women who were the first witnesses to the resurrection, and who then became apostles – 'sent' – to evangelise – 'tell good news' – to the male apostles.[10]

When a woman caught in adultery was brought to Jesus, his action condemned the men who brought her rather than the woman standing in front of him.[11] Jesus' prohibition of divorce might look harsh in our rather different context, but the intention appears to have been a law that would apply equally to men and women, and that would protect women's livelihoods, in preference to the traditional provision that gave all of the power to men.[12] And when Jesus visited two sisters, Mary and Martha, he treated Mary as a close follower, and offered her as a model to her sister Martha, who was rather too intent on performing the domestic activities expected of women.[13]

Jesus' attitude to women was typical of his attitude generally: everyone was welcome in the Kingdom of God, there would be no hierarchy, everyone would be treated the same, and everyone would be provided for. Both Isaiah and Jesus envisaged a Kingdom of God characterised by justice: the kind of justice described in the books of Deuteronomy and Leviticus. If we are followers of Jesus then we too will seek such a Kingdom, and we shall want to watch for and to create in our own society signs of the Kingdom's coming. This means that we will need to seek the kind of justice that Jesus envisaged: the kind of justice that provides for those in need, and that treats everyone the same.

At first sight this looks like a difficult combination to achieve, but in fact it isn't. The UK's National Health Service treats everyone the same, and it provides healthcare for those in need: and it does all of that more efficiently than any other OECD country's healthcare system.[14] The UK's Child Benefit treats every family the same (that is, every family with the same number of children receives the same amount of Child Benefit), and at the same time it provides a valuable income for families in need. It really does not matter that the wealthy don't need the Child Benefit that they receive. As far as poor families are concerned, the most valuable characteristic of Child Benefit is that it never stops (until the child is sixteen years old, or nineteen if they are still in full-time education). Other benefits might go down, or they might stop; earnings might gyrate as the weeks go by;[15] but Child Benefit just keeps on coming. Both Child Benefit and the National Health Service match precisely the kind of justice envisaged by the Jewish Law, and therefore by the prophets and by Jesus.

There is another sense in which Citizen's Basic Income is Jesus' kind of justice. 'An eye for an eye'[16] was perhaps more just than the revenge maimings and killings that preceded it; but Jesus wanted a whole new kind of justice:

> You have heard that it was said, 'An eye for an eye and a tooth for a tooth.' But I say to you … if anyone wants to sue you and take your coat, give your cloak as well; and if anyone forces you to go one mile, go also the second mile. Give to everyone who begs from you, and do not refuse anyone who wants to borrow from you.[17]

This is the kind of justice that a Citizen's Basic Income exercises. A Citizen's Basic Income takes no account of wrongs, antisocial behaviour, laziness, or anything else. This is a justice that ascribes a fundamental equality to every human being and then acts accordingly.

The kind of justice that we are here discussing is not far from the kind that John Rawls describes as 'justice as fairness' in his *A Theory of Justice*. In order to construct the kind of society that would embody his conception of justice, Rawls envisages an 'original position' in which all parties are equal: 'all have the same rights in the procedure for choosing principles' on which their society would be based. In this original position, Rawls posits a 'veil of ignorance': that is, he asks us to think of the citizens as not knowing which position they would hold in society, and then to choose the kind of society in which they would wish to live.[18]

In terms of income maintenance, would we want to live in a society in which everyone received the same income, or would we want to live in one in which we would be able to improve our financial situation if we chose to do so? If we might have dependants to care for, or we might want additional resources with which to serve our communities, or to do something else creative, we would choose a society in which we would be able to improve our financial position. We would therefore choose a society in which individuals with any initial income level would be able to improve their financial position relatively easily, and in which the poorest would find it particularly easy to do so – because we might be among the poorest in society. This suggests that behind Rawls' veil of ignorance we would choose a society in which everyone would be able to improve their own financial position, and in which this would be particularly true of the poorest.

This is not the society in which we live at the moment. In the UK we live in a society in which the wealthiest can improve their financial position by at least 53p for every extra £1 that they earn, and in which many of the near-poor can only improve their financial position by 4p for every extra £1 that they earn.[19] When Universal Credit replaces Working Tax Credits and Child Tax Credits, this will rise to 24p for every extra £1 earned, which will be an improvement, but it will still be well below the 53p available to the wealthy. This is not a society that we would choose behind Rawls' veil of ignorance. It is not a just society.

A Citizen's Basic Income of any amount would reduce the marginal deduction rates for anyone on means-tested benefits (including tax credits). (Depending on the details of the scheme, it might also increase income tax rates slightly, and so would mean anyone not on means-tested benefits experiencing a slightly higher withdrawal rate: but still nothing like the withdrawal rates suffered by those currently on means-tested benefits or tax credits.) A Citizen's Basic Income would therefore take us closer to a society in which everyone would be able to improve their financial position, and therefore closer to a just society.

A similar question relates to diversity. People are all different, and with different needs. Jesus faced this question when he was implicitly criticised by a Gentile woman for discriminating against Gentiles:

> From there he set out and went away to the region of Tyre. He entered a house and did not want anyone to know he was there. Yet he could not escape notice, but a woman whose little daughter had an unclean spirit immediately heard about him, and she came and bowed down at his feet. Now the woman was a Gentile, of Syrophoenician origin. She begged him to cast the demon out of her daughter. He said to her, 'Let the children be fed first, for it is not fair to take the children's food and throw it to the dogs.' But she answered him, 'Sir, even the dogs under the table eat the children's crumbs.' Then he said to her, 'For saying that, you may go – the demon has left your daughter.' So she went home, found the child lying on the bed, and the demon gone.[20]

It is perhaps this woman that we have to thank for Jesus' ministry to Gentiles,[21] for the Church's subsequent welcome to Gentile Christians, and for the meeting in Jerusalem at which the Church's leaders decided that Gentiles should not have to keep the Jewish Law but should instead only have to keep a brief set of rules that would ensure that Jewish Christians would not be scandalised.[22] Jesus' own vocation was to serve, not to be served;[23] increasingly his serving was without boundaries; and the Church learnt from him that there were to be no boundaries to its membership[24] or to its caring activity. It is from this history that the Church eventually learnt that slavery had to be abolished.

Whether we take our definition of justice from the Law, the prophets, and Jesus, or from John Rawls, we end up at the same position: a Citizen's Basic Income would deliver a society more just than a society with a benefits system based on means-tested benefits.

14.

Citizen's Basic Income would promote liberty

*And you shall hallow the fiftieth year and you shall proclaim
liberty throughout the land to all its inhabitants. It shall be
a jubilee for you: you shall return, every one of you, to your
property and every one of you to your family.*

(Leviticus 25: 10)

Whether the provisions relating to the year of jubilee recorded
in the book of Leviticus were actually carried out, or were
simply an expression of an imagined utopia, they offer us an
important connection: land being regularly returned to its original
occupants is described as 'liberty'. Liberty is not here understood
as someone's ability to choose their way of life, their occupation,
their relationships, or anything else. The liberty here described is
the provision of the economic basis for liberty. Having the use of
land, and therefore of its harvests, was what set people free from
oppression, free to bring up their families, and free to join in the life
of society. And so today: a sufficient income provides the basis for all
kinds of freedom: freedom to refuse a job, freedom to accept a low-
paying job, freedom to start a business, freedom to do voluntary or
caring work, freedom to be creative, freedom to seek skills, freedom
to research, freedom to form relationships, freedom to bring up a
family … . In today's society, some people have private incomes,
and those incomes set them free to pursue all manner of interests
and activities. As Sam Brittan, and more recently John O'Farrell

of the *Guardian*, have said, the only problem with private incomes is that not everybody has one.[1] To extend the privilege to every individual in society would massively enhance our collective and individual experiences of liberty.

When invited to read in the synagogue, Jesus read this passage from Isaiah:

> The spirit of the Lord God is upon me,
> because the Lord has anointed me;
> he has sent me to bring good news to the oppressed,
> to bind up the broken-hearted,
> to proclaim liberty to the captives,
> and release to the prisoners.[2]

He then told the congregation: 'Today this scripture has been fulfilled in your hearing'.[3] The Kingdom of God in which all would be healed and set free was a Kingdom that he embodied and a task to which he had committed himself. Those he met would find themselves set free from illness, possession, sin, guilt, and much else; and the liberty that they experienced would generate yet more liberty – the classic case being the tax collector Zaccheus: set free from his sin and guilt, he would now set free those whom he had exploited.[4]

Many of the earliest Christians experienced a liberation. They were Jews, and they knew that they had failed to keep God's law, as it was expressed in the first five books of the Old Testament – and that they would continue to fail to keep it. Jesus had sat lightly to the Law, and many of the earliest Christians had experienced his death and resurrection as a liberation from their old way of life and into a new era of freedom governed by Jesus' 'new commandment' to 'love one another'.[5] Early on there were Christians who still believed that as Jews they were obliged to keep the Law, and some of Jesus' sayings had suggested as much: but when non-Jews began to join the Church, and the apostles sensibly resisted a campaign to get Gentile Christians to keep the Jewish Law, the Church found itself heading away from the Jewish Law and into a new freedom.

But that had its own problems: and Paul had to deal with some of them in his letters to the Churches. One person's freedom could easily become someone else's oppression: and so in his letter to the Church in Galatia Paul urges Church members to use their new liberty to serve one another:

> For freedom Christ has set us free. Stand firm, therefore, and do not submit again to a yoke of slavery. … you were called to freedom, brothers and sisters; only do not use your freedom as an opportunity for self-indulgence, but through love become slaves to one another. For the whole law is summed up in a single commandment, 'You shall love your neighbour as yourself.'[6]

One thing that neither Paul nor any other Christian could do much about was slavery. It was part of the social fabric. The escape from Egypt that the enslaved Israelites had experienced, and the provisions in the Law for freeing slaves, would always have been in Christians' minds;[7] and in the Roman Empire slaves could sometimes buy their freedom: but when Paul was writing his letters, slavery was an embedded social institution that the powerless Christian Church could do little to change. In individual cases Paul did what he could (in his letter to Philemon he tried to persuade a master to set free a slave who had escaped and had found his way to Paul in Rome): but he could do nothing about the institution itself – although later, of course, Christians were at the heart of efforts to abolish both the slave trade and slavery. What Christians *could* do in New Testament times was ensure that in the context of the Church there would be no difference in status between slaves and free citizens:

> There is no longer Jew or Greek, there is no longer slave or free, there is no longer male and female; for all of you are one in Christ Jesus.[8]

Every individual Christian was 'in Christ', whatever their role in society. It is no surprise that slaves became Christians. The Church offered to them a liberty that they could find nowhere else.

It is this kind of liberty that we need to find in our society today: a liberty that exists alongside and contradicts the many oppressions that we experience in society. There are few social policies that achieve this. Free education does, giving to everybody access to the kind of training of the mind that can facilitate freedom of thought and action. A Citizen's Basic Income would achieve this as well. Not only would it provide a foundational economic security that would itself provide a basis for genuine liberty: freedom to form relationships, freedom to refuse lousy jobs, freedom to start a business, freedom to raise a family, and so on – but for many people it would also enable additional earnings to generate the additional disposable income that would increase those freedoms further.

And then we come to Paul's letter to the Romans:

> I consider that the sufferings of this present time are not worth comparing with the glory about to be revealed to us. For the creation waits with eager longing for the revealing of the children of God; for the creation was subjected to futility, not of its own will but by the will of the one who subjected it, in hope that the creation itself will be set free from its bondage to decay and will obtain the freedom of the glory of the children of God.[9]

Here is the most radical kind of freedom ever: freedom for the entire created order. The Kingdom of God 'has come near' in Jesus Christ,[10] but we still await its fulfilment. Any freedom that we experience today can only provide a mere hint of what such a freedom might look like: but if a Citizen's Basic Income can contribute just a little to our sense of freedom, then it will embody in our social fabric a promise of that greater freedom for which for now we can only hope.

It might be useful here to discuss a context in which freedom is exercised perhaps more than it once was: in the forming and dissolving of relationships. Because many women are now more financially independent than they once were, they are no longer forced to remain in an unhappy relationship by the prospect of poverty if they left it. Whatever we might think about the greater ease with which marriages and other long term relationships can be dissolved, an important positive advantage of a greater liberty to leave a relationship is an accompanying greater liberty to remain in it: for in the context of a freedom to leave, remaining becomes a genuine relationship choice. In the context of financial independence, remaining in a marriage can express both a commitment to a relationship and a commitment to marriage as a lifelong covenant, rather than being a decision enforced by economic necessity. In families in which one partner has no independent income, the advent of Citizen's Basic Income would provide the required independent income, and might therefore enhance the liberty experienced by that partner – a liberty to remain, as well as a liberty to leave.

Citizen's Basic Incomes would also give to people living separately a greater ability to choose to live together if that might be what they wanted to do. A lone parent on means-tested benefits (including tax credits) might hesitate to move in with someone else – either someone with their own earned income, or someone on means-tested benefits – because they would immediately lose their individual benefit income. Either they would find themselves making a joint claim for tax credits or out-of-work means-tested benefits, or their new partner's earnings would deprive them of the ability to make any claim at all for means-tested benefits. A Citizen's Basic Income would remove some or all of the disadvantages of choosing to live with someone else, and it would emphasise the advantages. Neither of the two individuals' Citizen's Basic Incomes would change if they decided to live together; there would often be less means-tested benefit for either partner to lose; and turning additional earnings into additional disposable income would be a lot easier. No longer would the benefits system be imposing disincentives to moving in together, so decisions as to whether to move in with someone else would be based on questions relating to the relationship rather than on the vagaries of the benefits system. Liberty would be enhanced.

There are two kinds of freedom: 'freedom from …', and 'freedom to …'. Freedom to form relationships on the basis of issues to do with the relationship would be improved by a Citizen's Basic Income: but a Citizen's Basic Income would also grant freedom from the kind of bureaucratic intrusion that accompanies means-tested benefits. Because in the UK two people living together receive less in means-tested benefits (including tax credits) than the two individuals would receive in total if they lived apart, the Department for Work and Pensions needs to know who is living with whom. Bureaucrats therefore need to explore the intimate details of the lives of people living in the same household. This is not the fault of the staff who do it. (I was once one of those staff members. We hated doing it.) It is entirely the fault of the system. Because a Citizen's Basic Income would be paid to each individual, no such intrusion would be required. Following the implementation of a Citizen's Basic Income scheme, if a family with sufficient earnings found itself with sufficient income to come off means-tested benefits, then they could escape entirely the bureaucratic intrusion, errors, overpayment demands, enquiries into changes in circumstances, and everything else that had bedevilled their lives. If a family still found itself on means-tested benefits after the implementation of a Citizen's Basic Income then they would usually be on less of them, and might be able to reduce their spending or add additional earned income in order to get off them – something that they might not have been able to do before. Their Citizen's Basic Incomes would thus grant a valuable 'freedom from': freedom from bureaucratic interference.

Means-tested benefits cannot help skewing people's relationships and interfering in them. A Citizen's Basic Income would neither skew nor interfere in relationships. Instead, it would increase people's choices, and would enable people to make relationship decisions based on factors more relevant to the relationships themselves. A Citizen's Basic Income would therefore be likely to increase relationship formation and survival rates, and also the quality of people's relationships.

In general, a Citizen's Basic Income would increase a lot of people's liberty, and would not reduce significantly anybody else's. At the point of implementation few families would experience the greater liberty of a significantly increased disposable income, but most would find themselves with a greater liberty to add to their disposable income with additional earnings. Slightly increased income tax rates might constrain choice slightly for some, but the constraint would be minimal compared to the greater liberty that would be experienced by so many others. For nobody would a Citizen's Basic Income remove every conceivable constraint, and freedom would never be complete: but if a Citizen's Basic Income might increase some people's liberty substantially while not decreasing significantly anybody else's, then it would be a rare kind of social policy, and it is high time that we gave it a try.[11]

We are all of us children of God, experiencing in a very partial way 'the freedom of the glory of the children of God':[12] a freedom that the whole created order will one day experience in its totality.[13] A Citizen's Basic Income and its effects would provide a glimpse of that freedom to come: so Christians in particular should be asking for Citizen's Basic Incomes for every member of society.

Luke's gospel records three parables with a similar theme. In the first, a sheep wanders away from the flock, and the shepherd abandons ninety-nine sheep in order to find it. In the second, a woman loses a coin, and she searches until she finds it. In the third, a son leaves home with his half of the inheritance, squanders it, and is then welcomed home by the father who had been waiting for him.[14] These are parables of escape, of the exercise of freedom: but freedom in a context of love and security, even if the one exercising their freedom does not always recognise that. Unconditional and universal social provision can provide a similar security within which we can exercise liberty. A Citizen's Basic Income would open new possibilities in relation to employment patterns, voluntary and caring work, and relationship-building. Without such a foundational security, freedom can be dangerous: but with a secure base we can become adventurous social and economic entrepreneurs. Such unconditional provision as a Citizen's Basic Income is a kind of social love: an embracing security within which freedom is not only safer and more possible, but within which it is positively encouraged.

15.

Citizen's Basic Income would both relativise and enhance the family

> *Then he said to them, 'You have a fine way of rejecting the commandment of God in order to keep your tradition! For Moses said, "Honour your father and your mother"; and, "Whoever speaks evil of father or mother must surely die." But you say that if anyone tells father or mother, "Whatever support you might have had from me is Corban" (that is, an offering to God) – then you no longer permit doing anything for a father or mother, thus making void the word of God through your tradition that you have handed on. And you do many things like this.'*
>
> (Mark 7:9–13)

Jesus' personal development is of course forever hidden from us, but it is possible to speculate. He might have started out as a follower of John the Baptist (he was, after all, baptised by him), and as a fierce advocate of a rigorous keeping of the Jewish Law: a 'radical', in the sense that he took people back behind the traditions that had grown up around the Law in order to return them to the heart of the matter, and in particular to the ten commandments. The passage above might be from that period. But then Jesus discovered his own intimate relationship with God, and his own authority – 'but I say to you ...'[1] – and he set about living and proclaiming a Kingdom of

God into which God invited lawkeeper and lawbreaker alike. The kernel of that Kingdom, and a sign of its coming, was the group of disciples that Jesus gathered and then sent out to preach and to heal as signs of the Kingdom's coming. It was this group of disciples that became the significant social institution for Jesus, relativising the status of his family: and the same would have been true for his followers. Whether this narrative of Jesus's own development is accurate or not, we find in the gospels both Jesus' teaching about the duty to care for one's parents and a relativising of natural family ties in relation to the Kingdom of God.

> Then [Jesus'] mother and his brothers came; and standing outside, they sent to him and called him. A crowd was sitting around him; and they said to him, 'Your mother and your brothers and sisters are outside, asking for you.' And he replied, 'Who are my mother and my brothers?' And looking at those who sat around him, he said, 'Here are my mother and my brothers! Whoever does the will of God is my brother and sister and mother.'[2]

And then Jesus went a step further:

> Whoever comes to me and does not hate father and mother, wife and children, brothers and sisters, yes, and even life itself, cannot be my disciple.[3]

Jesus here sets up a hierarchy between someone's following of him and their allegiance to their natural family: a hierarchy with some deep emotional content to it. But that does not mean that Jesus had given up on his family, nor they on him:

> Meanwhile, standing near the cross of Jesus were his mother, and his mother's sister, Mary the wife of Clopas, and Mary Magdalene. When Jesus saw his mother and the disciple whom he loved standing beside her, he said to his mother, 'Woman, here is your son.' Then he said to the disciple, 'Here

is your mother.' And from that hour the disciple took her into his own home.[4]

Jesus was still very involved with his family (which then would have meant the extended family, and not today's rather more restricted version). He remained attached to his mother; and his brother James became a leader in the Jerusalem Church, suggesting a continuing familial bond. Perhaps Jesus' own family were more involved in Jesus' three year ministry in Galilee, in his journey to Jerusalem, and in the development of the continuing movement that followed the first Easter Day, than the gospel writers are willing to let on.

So we find two attitudes side by side in the gospels: a valuing of the natural family, which we also find of course throughout the Old Testament and in the New Testament letters; and the Church as a new kind of family that relativises the importance of the natural family. The connection is the Kingdom of God, which relativises every current human relationship, including the community of Jesus' disciples.

How are we to translate the complex attitude to the family that we find in the gospels, and in the rest of the Old and New Testaments, into modern-day social policy? What seems to be required is policy that values the natural family but that also relativises it. But as we have seen, the relativising only goes so far: and when it comes to vulnerable members of one's family, they have to be cared for, as Jesus ensured that his mother would be cared for. The same is true of children. Jesus welcomed children, and he ascribed status to them in a somewhat countercultural manner; and he could not have been clearer that to damage a child deserved the most severe punishment.[5]

In the UK, only the family or household as a whole can make a claim for out-of-work or in-work means-tested benefits, so means-tested benefits treat the natural family as the only relevant social unit. At the same time, benefits administrators constantly interfere in the family's decision-making, thus compromising the family's autonomy. The UK's tax system is very different. Here it is the individual who is taxed, leaving individuals in a family to make their own financial arrangements with each other. While poverty among the elderly is now far less of a problem than it once was (due to older people's greater propensity to vote at General Elections, and therefore to governments having a strong incentive to maintain the value of state pensions), childhood poverty constitutes an increasingly serious problem in the UK and elsewhere.

While a Citizen's Basic Income would not solve every social problem (the housing crisis can only be solved by building more homes), it would help to ensure that elderly people and children were cared for. Each individual would receive their own Citizen's Basic Income, leaving individuals living in a family to make their own financial arrangements with each other. With some Citizen's Basic Income schemes, not every family would be taken off means-tested benefits, but every family would be a lot closer to coming off them, so a lot of families would choose to adjust their employment patterns and other financial arrangements in order to do so. Somewhat counterintuitively, by not choosing the family as the claimant unit, Citizen's Basic Incomes would be good for families.

Citizen's Basic Income would be particularly good for elderly people. In the UK we shall soon see a Single Tier State Pension – an increase in the Basic State Pension to the current level of the means-tested Pension Credit – which will take most pensioners off means-tested pensions and will therefore increase the incentive to save for retirement. Up until now, small private or occupational pensions have simply reduced the means-tested pensions on which many pensioners have had to rely. This has provided little incentive to save in private or occupational schemes. The new Single Tier State Pension will not be reduced if someone has savings or private or occupational pensions, so there will be far more incentive to make one's own financial provision for old age.

The situation would be similar for children. Most illustrative Citizen's Basic Income schemes envisage Child Citizen's Basic Incomes at levels higher than that of the current Child Benefit: so a family would find itself more able to provide for their children. At the same time, the fact that each individual adult would receive the same Citizen's Basic Income, whatever their employment pattern, would provide members of a family with more choice over how they organised their working lives: and, in particular, it would be easier for both parents in a two-parent household to work part-time rather than one working full time and the other not at all or for only a few hours a week. This would enable both parents to take additional time out of employment in order to care for children. Two substantial part-time employments would enable both parents to develop their careers, and would provide their children with a richer experience of parenting. All of this would considerably improve the situation of children in our society.[6]

Similarly, with Citizen's Basic Incomes providing a financial bedrock for a family's finances, caring for elderly people within the family would become easier. This does not mean that it would be easy (smaller homes are making it more difficult), and there will always be many factors involved in deciding the best way to care for frail elderly people: but it does mean that for many families there would be fewer financial reasons for deciding not to look after their elderly parents themselves, and that any member of a family who decided to dedicate time to the care of the elderly would still have an independent income.

The family is changing, and is becoming more diverse. The extended family is becoming less of a reality in people's lives as family members scatter in search of work, or because marriage partners now come from elsewhere in the country, or elsewhere in the world. There is now no 'typical family' of husband, wife, and children; and greater equality in relation both to gender and to sexual orientation has caused an explosion in different kinds of family structure. All of this means that 'the family' is no longer a useful idea on which to base social policy, if it ever was. For means-tested benefits regulations, everything other than the so-called typical family is an anomaly to be investigated. This is now an extreme anachronism. It is within the new diversity that the family must be resourced: and while we might not wish to incentivise family formation, we ought not to disincentivise it, as means-tested benefits regulations often do. The family as we currently find it needs support, because it is within the family that its members are cared for, and it is within the family that children learn social integration and personal and social skills. Only an individual-based income maintenance strategy can serve the complex current reality.

With a Citizen's Basic Income, individuals would be better able to form and to nurture families, and to turn their families into fellowships of individuals that would model the character of the Kingdom of God, of Jesus' fellowship of disciples, and of the Church. The family would be nurtured, and in particular its more vulnerable members would receive the care that they need.

16.

Citizen's Basic Income would facilitate the duty to serve

The alien who resides with you shall be to you as the citizen among you; you shall love the alien as yourself, for you were aliens in the land of Egypt: I am the Lord your God.
(Leviticus 19:34)

For whom should we care? Whom should we love? In John's gospel, Jesus' 'new commandment' is a command to 'love one another':[1] but this is rather less radical than the command in Leviticus to love the alien, and Jesus' command to love one's enemy.[2] We are to care for whoever crosses our paths. This is now rather more difficult to conceptualise in practical terms than it was in Jesus' time, because communications media bring the world to our computer and television screens – but the principle remains the same: we are to create no boundaries around those for whom we have a responsibility to care.

The Church that emerged on the Day of Pentecost after Jesus' resurrection faced this issue in very practical terms. Early on there was diversity in the Church. Gentiles – non-Jews – came later; but from the beginning there were Jews who spoke semitic languages (both Hebrew, for reading the Law and the Prophets, and Aramaic, which would have been Jesus' first disciples' mother tongue) and Jews who spoke Greek, the cosmopolitan language spoken around the eastern side of the Mediterranean. The Greek-speakers were complaining that their widows were being neglected, so the apostles established an organisation to ensure that they received their fair share.

> Now during those days, when the disciples were increasing in number, the Hellenists complained against the Hebrews because their widows were being neglected in the daily distribution of food. And the twelve called together the whole community of the disciples and said, 'It is not right that we should neglect the word of God in order to wait at tables. Therefore, friends, select from among yourselves seven men of good standing, full of the Spirit and of wisdom, whom we may appoint to this task, while we, for our part, will devote ourselves to prayer and to serving the word.'[3]

They were fulfilling their duty to serve by institutionalising their response, as Christians have frequently done,[4] and as we do when we donate to charities or establish foodbanks.

Underlying the love, the care, and the serving that we find in the New Testament, is Jesus' own servanthood:

> The Son of Man came not to be served but to serve, and to give his life a ransom for many.[5]

He did not discriminate, but gave his time both to the wealthy and to the most vulnerable, and performed his healing miracles for a leper and for a Roman centurion's servant[6] and for every social status in between. It is Jesus' servant ministry and the early Christians' serving of others that lie behind James's command to 'care for orphans and widows in their distress',[7] and behind one of William Temple's Christian principles: 'the duty to serve'.[8] We too must love, serve, and care, in highly practical terms. But how best to do that?

There are many ways in which each of us can serve: through employment, self-employment, voluntary activity, and care within the family. We can also pursue the kind of institutional response that the apostles tried when they found that a group of people were not being cared for. We might donate to charity, we might establish a new charity, or we might lobby for a change in how our country is run. All of these can fulfil our obligation to love and to serve.

One possibility, of course, is to promote debate on Citizen's Basic Income. We have seen how a Citizen's Basic Income would offer a number of benefits to individuals, to families, and to society as a whole. I shall not repeat them all here: but if we are persuaded that a Citizen's Basic Income might enhance the wellbeing of families and individuals in our society, then we ought to join in the debate and involve other people in it too. We do not need to be totally convinced of the case for Citizen's Basic Income to be able to do this: simply believing that it might have beneficial effects is sufficient to inspire us to put in a bit of effort to educate those who make decisions in the advantages and feasibilities of Citizen's Basic Income.

A particularly important effect of everyone receiving a Citizen's Basic Income would be everyone's increased ability to serve their communities, their families, and themselves, because everyone would be able to make different choices about their use of time – and the escape from bureaucratic control that many families would experience would release them from stigma and anxiety, and provide them with renewed energy to care for their community and for family members, to give a few more hours a week to serve unpaid in their church, charity shop, or local nature reserve, to take a gap year, or to take a few months between jobs to do full time volunteering. This particular characteristic of Citizen's Basic Income would turn our society into a signpost towards a Kingdom of God characterised by love and service: so for this reason alone Christians might wish to participate in the debate themselves and then persuade decision-makers to join in as well.

17.

Citizen's Basic Income would be welcoming and hospitable

The Lord appeared to Abraham by the oaks of Mamre, as he sat at the entrance of his tent in the heat of the day. He looked up and saw three men standing near him. When he saw them, he ran from the tent entrance to meet them, and bowed down to the ground. He said, 'My lord, if I find favour with you, do not pass by your servant. Let a little water be brought, and wash your feet, and rest yourselves under the tree. Let me bring a little bread, that you may refresh yourselves, and after that you may pass on — since you have come to your servant.'

(Genesis 18:1–5)

The three messengers had come with a message to Abraham: that his elderly wife Sarah was to bear a child. After they left Abraham they visited his nephew Lot, who welcomed and protected them. Hospitality became a core principle of the Jewish religion. Anyone travelling through was to be welcomed and fed: a principle that survived into the early Church, although the Letter to the Hebrews suggests that Christians might have needed to be reminded of this:

> Let mutual love continue. Do not neglect to show hospitality to strangers, for by doing that some have entertained angels without knowing it.[1]

Hospitality has always been a core principle of the monastic orders, and today there are Christians who will give a bed to a young person who suddenly finds themselves homeless, or who will house newly arrived asylum seekers … .

According to Matthew's gospel, Jesus' parents first of all fulfilled prophecy by going to Bethlehem so that Jesus the Messiah would be born there – 'But you, O Bethlehem of Ephrathah, who are one of the little clans of Judah, from you shall come forth for me one who is to rule in Israel …';[2] and then, to escape Herod's massacre of the children of Bethlehem, they took the infant Jesus into Egypt. They were refugees, welcomed into a foreign country, and then welcomed into a different part of their own.[3] Throughout his ministry, Jesus was constantly welcomed into people's homes;[4] and, although he appears to have had no home of his own, his attitude was always one of unconditional welcome – often while accepting other people's hospitality. Jesus' parable of the Good Samaritan[5] tells of a foreigner who shows hospitality to an injured Jew. For Jesus, there were no boundaries. Hospitality can be exercised by anyone, and can be received by anyone. The 'neighbour' can be anyone at all.

All of this raises interesting questions in relation both to Church governance and to a Citizen's Basic Income. Some of those questions are easier to answer than others. In relation to children: somewhat unusually for his time, Jesus treated children as people in their own right. They were not simply future adults: they were individuals, and no one was going to stop them from meeting Jesus.

> Then little children were being brought to him in order that he might lay his hands on them and pray. The disciples spoke sternly to those who brought them; but Jesus said, 'Let the little children come to me, and do not stop them; for it is to such as these that the kingdom of heaven belongs.' And he laid his hands on them and went on his way.[6]

The care and safety of children was one of Jesus' primary concerns; and he reserved his harshest judgement for those whose practice did not conform to the highest standards of care: 'If any of you put a stumbling-block before one of these little ones who believe in me, it would be better for you if a great millstone were hung around your neck and you were thrown into the sea.' [7] Within a few years Paul was baptising the Philippian jailer 'and his entire family': [8] and although there have always been some Churches that have declined to baptise infants, there have always been Churches that baptise children, enabling them to belong to the Church just as much as adults do. A constant tension has been the result: between the requirement that membership of the Church is an act of God's grace, and the insistence that a freely chosen confession of faith is required. Hence a series of compromises: first of all the requirement of an adult confession of faith at 'confirmation' before admission to communion; and the more recent admission of children to communion at the age of seven following a series of classes. Jesus' own practice suggests that compromise is not required, and that everyone present at the Eucharist should be invited to participate in the same way. A hospitable God implies a Church that offers an unconditional welcome.

The same tension is evident in relation to most benefits systems. There will often be a statement of universality – for instance, of social security being a citizenship right: but then a series of conditions that have to be fulfilled before payment can be received. Abraham did not question the three messengers' credentials: he sat them down and had a meal prepared for them. If we were to model our benefits system on Abraham's and Jesus' hospitality then everyone present in the country would receive an income without any conditions having to be fulfilled. This raises a number of questions: Should prisoners receive the same Citizen's Basic Income as everyone else? Should asylum seekers? Should temporary visitors receive Citizen's Basic Incomes? And in relation to a rather toxic current debate: Should EU citizens receive Citizen's Basic Incomes as soon as they arrive in the UK?

The answer to each of these questions has to be 'yes'. In relation to short term prisoners, there would be an argument for saving up their Citizen's Basic Incomes to provide them with funds on their release. For longer term prisoners, there would be an argument for using some of their Citizen's Basic Incomes for the same purpose, and for the rest to contribute towards the cost of their board and lodging in prison. In relation to migrant workers there is no problem. The problem with the current means-tested benefits system is that it discourages recipients from seeking employment. A Citizen's Basic Income would not have this effect, and so would be preferable to the current system: and because everyone in the country would be receiving a Citizen's Basic Income, there would be no sense that a worker who had just arrived in the country would be receiving something that longstanding residents were not receiving.

Hospitality – an unconditional welcome – is at the heart of the Christian Faith. Hospitality – an unconditional welcome – is at the heart of Citizen's Basic Income. The Christian Faith and Citizen's Basic Income clearly belong together.

Paying for a Citizen's Basic Income

Set apart a tithe of all the yield of your seed that is brought in yearly from the field. In the presence of the Lord your God, in the place that he will choose as a dwelling for his name, you shall eat the tithe of your grain, your wine, and your oil, as well as the firstlings of your herd and flock, so that you may learn to fear the Lord your God always. ... Every third year you shall bring out the full tithe of your produce for that year, and store it within your towns; the Levites, because they have no allotment or inheritance with you, as well as the resident aliens, the orphans, and the widows in your towns, may come and eat their fill so that the Lord your God may bless you in all the work that you undertake.

(Deuteronomy 14:22–29)

Taxation goes back a long way. In the tithing regulations we find taxation to provide for community celebration and for the sustenance of those without land of their own; and in the Sabbath regulations we find a kind of lifecycle taxation: putting goods aside so that they can be used later on.

For six years you shall sow your field, and for six years you shall prune your vineyard, and gather in their yield; but in the seventh year there shall be a sabbath of complete rest for the land, a sabbath for the Lord: you shall not sow your field or prune your vineyard. ... Should you ask, 'What shall we eat in the seventh year, if we may not sow or gather in our crop?' I will order my blessing for you in the sixth year, so that it will yield a crop for three years. When you sow in the eighth year, you will be eating from the old crop; until the ninth year, when its produce comes in, you shall eat the old.[1]

Jesus' criticism of some of the taxation practices of his own time – 'Woe to you, scribes and Pharisees, hypocrites! For you tithe mint, dill, and cummin, and have neglected the weightier matters of the law: justice and mercy and faith. It is these you ought to have practised without neglecting the others. You blind guides! You strain out a gnat but swallow a camel!'[2] – was not a criticism of tithes: it was a criticism of the injustice that they practised, of which the story of the widow's mite might be an example:

[Jesus] sat down opposite the treasury, and watched the crowd putting money into the treasury. Many rich people put in large sums. A poor widow came and put in two small copper coins, which are worth a penny. Then he called his disciples and said to them, 'Truly I tell you, this poor widow has put in more than all those who are contributing to the treasury. For all of them have contributed out of their abundance; but she out of her poverty has put in everything she had, all she had to live on.'[3]

The more traditional commentaries treat this passage as a moral tale: Jesus is commending the woman for her generosity, and is comparing it with the rather less generous contributions of the rich.[4] But there is another interpretation: that onerous taxation was depriving the poor of their livelihoods, whereas the wealthy were having to pay a rather smaller proportion of their abundance.[5]

Was Jesus opposed to taxation? When challenged about the legitimacy of Jews paying taxes to the Roman occupiers, he asked to be brought a coin:

> Then he said to them, 'Whose head is this, and whose title?'
> They answered, 'The emperor's.' Then he said to them, 'Give
> therefore to the emperor the things that are the emperor's,
> and to God the things that are God's.'[6]

– and whatever we make of an incident relating to the Jewish
temple tax, it yields an equally ambiguous message:

> When they reached Capernaum, the collectors of the temple
> tax came to Peter and said, 'Does your teacher not pay the
> temple tax?' He said, 'Yes, he does.' And when he came home,
> Jesus spoke of it first, asking, 'What do you think, Simon?
> From whom do kings of the earth take toll or tribute? From
> their children or from others?' When Peter said, 'From others',
> Jesus said to him, 'Then the children are free. However, so
> that we do not give offence to them, go to the lake and cast
> a hook; take the first fish that comes up; and when you open
> its mouth, you will find a coin; take that and give it to them
> for you and me.'[7]

Jesus seems to have made friends with plenty of tax collectors, one
of whom, Matthew, became a close follower;[8] and when Jesus met
Zacchaeus the tax collector, the outcome was a promise to more
than compensate those from whom he had extorted too much:[9]
but there is no suggestion that any of these tax-collectors ceased to
collect taxes. Jesus' life and message was about a Kingdom of God
that both now and in the future will sweep aside the exploitative
ways in which we organise our life together. Until then, the weeds
must grow in among the wheat. Only at 'harvest time', when the
Kingdom of God finally comes, will the harvesters gather the weeds
before collecting the wheat into God's barn.[10] In the meantime, we
must 'give to God the things that are God's',[11] and free ourselves
from everything that hinders us from entering God's Kingdom:

No one can serve two masters; for a slave will either hate the one and love the other, or be devoted to the one and despise the other. You cannot serve God and wealth.[12]

For a rich young man, that meant giving away his wealth:

Jesus, looking at him, loved him and said, 'You lack one thing; go, sell what you own, and give the money to the poor, and you will have treasure in heaven; then come, follow me.' When he heard this, he was shocked and went away grieving, for he had many possessions.[13]

As we have seen, the earliest Christians did as they were asked, and disposed of their assets: but this could only happen once, and because the Kingdom of God did not immediately arrive they had to be helped out by Christians elsewhere.[14] Clearly a longer term strategy was required: but if Christians were to live as normal citizens, earning incomes and caring for assets, then they would have to come to a view on the legitimacy of taxation. Paul was a Roman citizen, never seemed to have a problem with Roman authority, and by the time he wrote his letter to the Christians in Rome his positive theology of secular authority had delivered a verdict in favour of taxation:

Let every person be subject to the governing authorities; for there is no authority except from God, and those authorities that exist have been instituted by God. ... For the same reason you also pay taxes, for the authorities are God's servants, busy with this very thing. Pay to all what is due to them – taxes to whom taxes are due, revenue to whom revenue is due, respect to whom respect is due, honour to whom honour is due.[15]

There would have been no thought then of paying a Citizen's Basic Income to every resident of the Roman empire, or to every Roman citizen: but if there had been then Jesus would have been comfortable with a fair income tax to pay for it, and Paul would have been positively enthusiastic.

But is income the best thing to tax? Work – whether paid or unpaid – is God-given and a source of dignity: 'The Lord God took the man and put him in the garden of Eden to till it and keep it'[16] – but it can also be exploitative and demeaning. If we tax something then we make it more expensive, which tends to reduce its supply. If we tax paid employment then we are likely to reduce the amount of paid employment. This suggests that we should tax lousy jobs but not good jobs – although it would be impracticable to do that. For the foreseeable future, paid employment will be an important means of providing individuals and households with the income that they need, so we probably ought not to tax earned income more than we have to. On the other hand, income tax can redistribute from rich to poor if we choose allowances and rates appropriately. This suggests that income tax rates should generally be low, but that higher rates should be charged on higher earnings; and that the UK's National Insurance Contributions, which tax low earned income at 12 per cent, and higher earned income at just 2 per cent, is not the kind of tax that Christians would wish to commend.

What we ought to be taxing, of course, is not paid work, but the 'bads' that we want to discourage. We tax smoking because we want to discourage it, and because smoking imposes costs on publicly funded health services. We tax alcohol in order to reduce its consumption, and, again, to contribute to healthcare costs related to alcohol abuse. The scriptures regard the care of our bodies as a spiritual issue:

> Do you not know that your body is a temple of the Holy Spirit within you, which you have from God, and that you are not your own? For you were bought with a price; therefore glorify God in your body.[17]

> Do not get drunk with wine, for that is debauchery; but be filled with the Spirit.[18]

– so Christians should have a particular interest in taxing practices that damage our bodies. The UK's new tax on drinks with high sugar content is a step in the right direction.

Our vocation as stewards of God's creation – 'the Lord God took the man and put him in the garden of Eden to till it and keep it'[19] – suggests another theologically appropriate tax. Carbon emissions are polluting the planet's atmosphere and warming the climate, perhaps disastrously. Carbon emissions are a planetary 'bad', so it would be entirely appropriate to tax carbon use. This would reduce the amount of carbon used, and at the same time would provide a stream of revenue that could be used to mitigate the consequences of climate change. Because fuel prices might rise, it would also be appropriate to use the proceeds to pay for a Citizen's Basic Income so that households could continue to afford to heat their homes. If we were to tax carbon use and apply some of the proceeds to investment in renewable energy, then the costs of heating our buildings might fall. To tax carbon use and apply the proceeds to a Citizen's Basic Income, to investment in renewable energy, and to the mitigation of climate change consequences, could be a most useful comprehensive approach.

One of the reasons that taxing earned income might not be a good idea is that paid employment is 'elastic': that is, if the price goes up then the supply goes down. If we tax paid employment, then there will be less of it – and therefore less to tax. A better kind of tax might be a tax on something that will always be in constant supply. Land is the obvious example. Apart from the occasional coastal erosion, land reclamation, or changes in countries' boundaries, a country's landmass will always be the same: so taxing land will not alter the supply of land. The idea has good theological warrant:

> The Lord spoke to Moses on Mount Sinai, saying ... the land shall not be sold in perpetuity, for the land is mine; with me you are but aliens and tenants.[20]

So however much of a 'freehold' we think we might possess, the land is God's. Thus the Leviticus 'jubilee' laws[21] provide for the return of land to the original owners once every fifty years, and define a just sale price in terms of the number of harvests that will be reaped before the next year of jubilee. Whether Israel ever kept these rules is debatable, but the theology is correct; and a secular version of it – that the land belongs to everyone, and that anyone who occupies land should therefore compensate those who don't occupy land – is what motivated Thomas Paine's suggestion that a tax on land should pay for an unconditional income for 'every person, rich or poor … because it is in lieu of the natural inheritance, which, as a right, belongs to every man … .'[22] Determining the value that accrues to those who occupy land is no easy matter, so it would not be easy to calculate the amount of tax that each occupant of land should pay: but the principle is correct. Land should be taxed because it belongs to everyone, and because taxing it would not reduce the amount of land available to be taxed.

There are thus a number of practical and theologically appropriate ways to raise the revenue required to pay for Citizen's Basic Incomes for every member of a country's population. Equally practical would be a financial transaction tax: that is, a tax on currency exchange. A useful funding method that now looks a lot more feasible than it once did is government money creation. Recent quantitative easing has enabled governments to buy government bonds, which has reduced their supply and benefited their owners; whereas to use government money creation to pay for a Citizen's Basic Income would benefit everyone, would increase consumption of goods and services, would increase employment, and would only increase inflation if the amount of money created was greater than the gap between the amount of money in circulation and the productive capacity of the economy. The proceeds of production are increasingly ending up with the owners of capital rather than in wages, so there is plenty of scope for using government money creation to fill the gap between the total productive capacity of the economy and the proportion paid out in wages. Financial transaction taxes and quantitative easing are not financial mechanisms for which we shall find obvious scriptural references, but that is no reason not to pursue them if they could usefully fund a Citizen's Basic Income, which, as we have seen, possesses plenty of theological justification.

Taxation is a theological issue, and Citizen's Basic Income is a theological issue. Both Citizen's Basic Income, and the means by which we might pay for it, are entirely proper issues for Christians to discuss – and to discuss theologically as well as in relation to a Citizen's Basic Income's desirabilities and feasibilities.

As David says when he dedicates the gifts that the people of Israel have contributed to the building of the temple:

> All things come from you, and of your own have we given you. … O Lord our God, all this abundance that we have provided for building you a house for your holy name comes from your hand and is all your own.[23]

We are able to pay tax because we have received what we have as a gift; and, as long as the tax is fair and just, we gladly pay it for the benefit of ourselves, of others, and of the world that God has lent to us. To pay tax of a variety of kinds in order to fund a Citizen's Basic Income would be a doubly Christian thing to do.

19.

Citizen's Basic Income would be an act of love

Beloved, let us love one another, because love is from God;
everyone who loves is born of God and knows God. Whoever
does not love does not know God, for God is love. God's love
was revealed among us in this way: God sent his only Son
into the world so that we might live through him. In this is
love, not that we loved God but that he loved us and sent his
Son to be the atoning sacrifice for our sins. Beloved, since God
loved us so much, we also ought to love one another.

(1 John 4:7–11)

The order is easy to state. First of all, God's love for us: and then, because God has loved us, we are called to love – with a love defined by God's love. So Jesus gives to his followers a command to love:

> I give you a new commandment, that you love one another. Just as I have loved you, you also should love one another. By this everyone will know that you are my disciples, if you have love for one another.[1]

So our love for one another is defined and inspired by Jesus' love for us – which is God's love for us.

And then Paul (who might have been making use of a passage about love already doing the rounds of the Churches) lists the characteristics of love.

> Love is patient; love is kind; love is not envious or boastful or arrogant or rude. It does not insist on its own way; it is not irritable or resentful; it does not rejoice in wrongdoing, but rejoices in the truth. It bears all things, believes all things, hopes all things, endures all things.[2]

If we read the three passages above together, then the love that Paul talks about describes both God's love for us and the love that we are called to have for each other. It is a highly practical love: a set of actions that together constitute love. There is nothing sentimental or romantic here. It's all about what we do. God's love is patient, kind, not envious or boastful or arrogant or rude. It does not insist on its own way; it is not irritable or resentful; it does not rejoice in wrongdoing, but rejoices in the truth. It bears all things, believes all things, hopes all things, endures all things. And it is this kind of love that we are called to exercise.

Can love be institutional? Why not? If an institution is patient, kind, not envious or boastful or arrogant or rude; does not insist on its own way; is not irritable or resentful; does not rejoice in wrongdoing, but rejoices in the truth; bears all things, believes all things, hopes all things, and endures all things: then that institution is exercising love. On this basis, there is not much that is loving about means-tested benefits. They are impatient to know their claimants' changes of circumstances, to get claimants into employment, or to get them into more employment; and they are not very kind as a claimant looks for employment, or when they are disabled or ill. Means-tested benefits are envious of claimants' savings and earnings; they claim to be the solution for poverty, when they are not; they will not hear of criticism; they are demeaning and stigmatising; they insist on their own complicated regulations; they are irritable about tentative personal relationships; they resent other kinds of benefits; they prosecute claimant error; they rejoice at detected wrongdoing; their regulations are obscure, and they ignore the fact that those regulations disincentivise employment; their sanctions can be rapid and unthinking; they require detailed evidence of claimants' circumstances; the only hope that they offer is of more of the same; and they put up with nothing.

Citizen's Basic Income, on the other hand, just keeps on coming, whatever is going on in someone's life; and the generosity goes on and on, from birth to death. Citizen's Basic Income has no problem with someone's earnings or savings; it blends into the background as a secure foundation on which to build; it never imposes conditions; it never criticises recipients; there are no regulations to insist on; it never interferes in personal relationships; it works happily alongside other benefits; there can be no error to rejoice in; it could not be more transparent; there are no sanctions to apply; it never requires evidence of changes of circumstance; it encourages recipients to seek new skills, new relationships, and better jobs; and it can put up with anything that anyone throws at it.

So Citizen's Basic Income is a superb example of institutional love – of 'love at a distance'[3] – and, like the love of God that inspires our love for one another, the love that Citizen's Basic Income exercises would motivate love in its recipients. Citizen's Basic Income would encourage care work, voluntary community work, and good jobs in place of lousy jobs; and it would enable a lot of individuals to turn additional earned income into additional disposable income, and so would make it easier for them to provide for their dependents. Citizen's Basic Income would therefore enable people to love more easily; and the love that it would facilitate would be the kind that Paul discussed in his letter to the Church in Corinth.

Citizen's Basic Income recipients would be more patient, because they would be able to look for the right new job rather than rushing into any new job. It would enable them add to their disposable income, and might enable them to organise their time so that they could exercise more kindness. Everyone would receive a Citizen's Basic Income, so there would be no cause for envy; no one would earn their Citizen's Basic Income, so there would be nothing to boast about; no one would be able to say that other people received benefits, but that they worked for their income, because everyone would receive a Citizen's Basic Income, and paid work would be more equally shared; and no one would be able to ridicule someone for receiving their Citizen's Basic Income. Everyone would have more choice over their employment pattern and their use of time, so no one would be able to impose their employment pattern on anyone else. Everyone's enhanced financial security would reduce anxiety; nobody would receive more Citizen's Basic Income than someone else of the same age, so there would be nothing to resent. There would be no error or fraud, so there would be no wrongdoing to rejoice in; and everyone would know exactly how much Citizen's Basic Income everyone else received. Anxiety relating to sanctions, bureaucratic inefficiency, and failure to report changes in circumstances, would not apply: so there would be much more emotional energy available to cope with everything else that might be changing. There would be no cause for suspicion that someone else might be receiving more than they should; and there would be so much to hope for: time for caring, time for volunteering, a better job, more skills, and an intimate relationship that would not be compromised by benefits problems. Above all, a Citizen's Basic Income recipient would experience a firm financial floor that nothing could shift, and so would be able to cope with all manner of financial, employment, and relationship changes that would previously have had serious consequences for their disposable income. There might still be consequences, but nothing would compromise their Citizen's Basic Income. They would be able to endure.

So a Citizen's Basic Income would be an act of love that would invite answering acts of love from its recipients: just as God's love for us invites answering acts of love from us.

For Jesus, for Paul, and therefore for us, love is action. Love is what we do. If we are patient, kind, not envious or boastful or arrogant or rude, do not insist on our own way, are not irritable or resentful, do not rejoice in wrongdoing, rejoice in the truth, bear all things, believe all things, hope all things, and endure all things, then that is love. And if Citizen's Basic Income is all of those things, then that too is an act of love.

Conclusion: Citizen's Basic Income: A Christian Social Policy

The conclusion can be briefly stated.

Citizen's Basic Income would celebrate God-given abundance, be an act of grace, recognise our individuality, recognise God's equal treatment of us, provide for the poor, not judge, constantly forgive, ensure that workers would be paid for their work, be the basis of a covenant, inspire us to be co-creators, understand both our original righteousness and our original corruption, recognise our mutual dependency, facilitate a more just society, promote liberty, both relativise and enhance the family, facilitate the duty to serve, be welcoming and hospitable, and be an act of love. Citizen's Basic Income is a Christian social policy, and perhaps the most Christian social policy possible. The methods by which we might pay for Citizen's Basic Incomes could be equally Christian.

Let the debate continue.

Appendix 1

Two feasible illustrative Citizen's Basic Income schemes for the UK[1]

The Citizen's Basic Income schemes studied here assume the rates shown in table 1:

Table 1: Citizen's Basic Income amounts in 2013/14 for the two illustrative schemes

	Scheme A	Scheme B
Relationship of Citizen's Basic Income to means-tested benefits **CBIs per week**	Citizen's Basic Incomes replace means-tested benefits except for Housing Benefit and Council Tax Support. Child Benefit and Basic State Pension are no longer paid.	Means-tested benefits are left in place and CBIs are taken into account when means-tested benefits are calculated. Basic State Pension and Child Benefit still paid.
Citizen's Pension (over 65)	£145.40	£30 (+ Basic State Pension)
Working age adult CBI (25 to 64)	£71.70	£54.20
Young adult CBI (16 to 24)	£56.80	£40
Child CBI	£56.80	£20 (+ Child Benefit)

Paying for the two schemes

- *First step*: If means-tested and other benefits are abolished, then the savings made can be used to fund Citizen's Basic Incomes. If means-tested benefits are reduced by taking into account people's Citizen's Basic Incomes when they are calculated, then again there will be savings, and these can be used to pay for Citizen's Basic Incomes. We can assume administrative savings of £4bn per annum where means-tested benefits are abolished, and £1bn per annum where they are retained (because everyone will have their means-tested benefits reduced by the total of Citizen's Basic Incomes received by the household, so fewer people will be receiving means-tested benefits).

- *Second step*: Currently Employees' National Insurance Contributions are regressive: that is, people with high earnings pay only 2 per cent of any additional earnings, whereas people with lower earnings pay 12 per cent of any additional earnings. These rates could be equalised at 12 per cent; and, because each individual would be receiving a Citizen's Basic Income, we could remove the Lower Earnings Limit, with the effect that National Insurance Contributions would be paid at 12 per cent on all earnings.

- *Third step*: Personal Income Tax Allowances would be abolished. If there is still a funding gap, then Income Tax rates can be raised to provide the additional revenue required.

Table 2 shows the tax rates required to fund the two illustrative schemes, and the number of losses that would be experienced by households at the point of implementation.

The financial feasibilities of the illustrative schemes²

Table 2: Citizen's Basic Income amounts in 2013/14 for the illustrative schemes, increases in tax rates to fund the schemes, and losses at the point of implementation

	Scheme A	**Scheme B**
Relationship of Citizen's Basic Income to means-tested benefits **CBIs per week**	Citizen's Basic Incomes replace means-tested benefits except for Housing Benefit and Council Tax Support. Child Benefit and State Pension are no longer paid.	Means-tested benefits are left in place and CBIs are taken into account when means-tested benefits are calculated. Basic State Pension and Child Benefit are still paid.
Citizen's Pension	£145.40	£30 (+State Pension)
Working age adult CBI	£71.70	£54.20
Young adult CBI	£56.80	£40
Child CBI	£56.80	£20 (+ Child Ben.)
Increase in Income Tax rates required	5%	3.5%
Proportion of households experiencing losses of over 10% at the point of implementation		
Households in the lowest income decile	28.03%	1.47% (and 3.78% with losses over 5%)
All households	15.2%	1.48% (and 12.40% with losses over 5%)

To increase Income Tax rates by 5 per cent might not be feasible. Also, scheme A would impose high losses on many households, including poor ones. Scheme A would therefore not be financially feasible in the short term, although it might be feasible in the longer term if additional funding became available.

Scheme B would raise Income Tax rates by 3.5 per cent and would impose few losses. It would be financially feasible in the short term, and it could be implemented almost overnight. It would pay genuine Citizen's Basic Incomes that would transform the lives of many households, because even though it would not take everyone off means-tested benefits straight away, it would take a lot of households off means-tested benefits, and it would leave many households within striking distance of coming off them and therefore able to do so. The detailed results can be found in table 3.

Housing costs

The Citizen's Basic Income schemes outlined here do not pretend to solve the housing crisis, which is why in both schemes Housing Benefit is retained. We are aware that housing-related benefits need radical simplification and reform, but that is a separate debate and not directly related to the implementation of a Citizen's Basic Income scheme. Housing benefits are usually paid to households whereas it is fundamental to a Citizen's Basic Income that it is paid to individuals.

Similarly, Council Tax Support is retained. This is now locally regulated as well as locally administered.

Implementation methods

There are several options for implementing a Citizen's Basic Income Scheme:

- *All at once*: On the chosen day, each individual would be paid their Citizen's Basic Income, means-tested benefits would be abolished or recalculated, Income Tax Personal Allowances would be reduced, and adjustments would be made to National Insurance Contribution rates.
- *One age group at a time*: The process could start by turning Child Benefit into a genuine Child Citizen's Basic Income by equalising the amounts paid to the first and to the second and subsequent children in the family, and by increasing its value; or by adding a small Child Citizen's

Table 3: Households taken off means-tested benefits, or taken to within £30 per week of coming off them.

	Tax Credits (Working Tax Credit and/or Child Tax Credit)	Out-of-work means-tested benefits: Income-related Job-seeker's Allowance, Income Support, Pension Credit [1]
% of households claiming means-tested benefits in 2013 under the current scheme	20.36	11.92
% of households claiming means-tested benefits under the CI scheme B	17.03	7.21
% reduction in households claiming means-tested benefits	16.31	39.57
% of all households claiming more than £30 per week in means-tested benefits under the current scheme	17.50	11.06
% of all households claiming more than £30 per week in means-tested benefits under the CI scheme	15.02	1.69
% reduction in households claiming more than £30 per week in means-tested benefits	14.17	84.47

[1] EUROMOD, the microsimulation programme managed by the Institute for Social and Economic Research and used to generate the results in this appendix, does not disaggregate these benefits when it reports household outcomes. Because of the complexity of the UK's method for maintain incomes during illness and maternity (statutory sickness and maternity pay and contributory and means-tested benefits) I have not attempted to evaluate the Citizen's Basic Income scheme's likely impact on incomes during illness and maternity.

Basic Income to a retained Child Benefit. Secondly, the new Single Tier State Pension could be turned into a Citizen's Pension by removing the link with National Insurance Contribution records. Thirdly, a Preretirement Citizen's Basic Income could be given to individuals over the age of say 55. Fourthly, a Young Adult Citizen's Basic Income could then be implemented. Finally, a Citizen's Basic Income for working age adults would fill the gap in the middle.

- *An evolutionary approach*: This process too would start by implementing a Child Citizen's Basic Income and a Citizen's Pension. Then would come a Young Adult Citizen's Basic Income for sixteen year olds. As each single year cohort of young adults grew older they would retain their Citizen's Basic Incomes and would not receive Income Tax Personal Allowances. By this method it would take about fifty years to complete the process.

- *A voluntary approach*: Once a Child Citizen's Basic Income, a Citizen's Pension, and a Young adult Citizen's Basic Income had been established, individuals could be invited to swap their Income Tax Personal Allowances for Citizen's Basic Incomes.

Redistribution

Figure 1 shows the aggregate redistribution that would occur if the Citizen's Basic Income scheme based on a working age adult Citizen's Basic Income of £54.20 and scheme B above were to be implemented.

Figure 1: Increase in disposable income by earnings decile on the implementation of a Citizen's Basic Income based on a working age adult's Citizen's Basic Income of £54.20 per week. (Decile 1 is the poorest 10% of households in terms of disposable income, and decile 10 is the wealthiest)

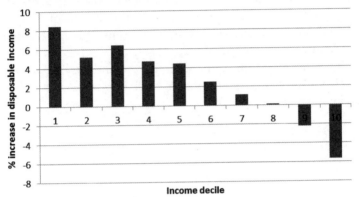

Because the only changes required to implement the scheme described here would be:

- payment of the Citizen's Basic Incomes (calculated purely in relation to the age of each individual)
- changes to Income Tax and National Insurance Contribution rates and thresholds
- easy to achieve recalculations in existing means–tested benefits claims this scheme could be implemented very quickly.

Conclusion

A strictly revenue neutral scheme with a working age adult Citizen's Basic Income set at £54.20 per week in 2013 would have imposed very few losses at the point of implementation, would have redistributed somewhat from rich to poor, would have increased Income Tax rates by only 3.5 per cent, and would have reduced substantially both the numbers of claims for in-work and out-of-work means-tested benefits and the amounts of those benefits paid to households. With a Citizen's Basic Income scheme of this type, a significant number of households would no longer be receiving Tax Credits, and an equally significant number of households would no longer be claiming over £30 per week. There would be a precipitous fall in the number of claims for out-of-work means-tested benefits, and almost no households would be claiming over £30 per week.

The impact of this quite conservative and easy to achieve Citizen's Basic Income scheme on both employment incentives and poverty would be both positive and considerable.

Appendix 2

Alternative options for the reform of the UK's tax and benefits system[1]

Tax Credits

(Real ones: not what the Government calls 'tax credits'.)

A credit is allocated to every individual. If someone is earning nothing, then the credit is paid. As earnings rise, the credit is withdrawn. At the point at which the credit is exhausted, Income Tax starts to be paid.

Tax credits can be administered by the Government or by the employer. If the Government administers the scheme, then the employer must provide information on earnings to the Government, as with the current Universal Credit. If the employer administers the scheme, then if someone moves from one employer to another then their Tax Credit administration has to move with them. If they have a period of unemployment, then the employer has to hand administration of their Tax Credits to the Government and then the Government has to hand it on to the new employer. If a worker is employed by two separate employers then the employers have to decide which of them will administer the Tax Credit; and if a worker has self-employed earnings as well then their employer needs to be informed so that the right amount of Tax Credit can be withdrawn.

Some Tax Credit schemes allocate different levels of Credit to people in different circumstances: for instance, a larger credit for a married couple. This adds another layer of complexity, because both the employer and the Government will need to know the workers' circumstances in order to calculate the correct Tax Credit.

With Tax Credits, each month some of the allocated Tax Credit has to be paid out, or Income Tax has to be collected. This will only work if there is a single tax rate: so anyone paying higher rate tax would need to pay additional Income Tax at the end of the tax year.

Negative Income Tax

A Negative Income Tax scheme functions in the same way as genuine Tax Credits. The only difference is in how the scheme is described. For a Tax Credit scheme, the amount to be paid out if there are no earnings has to be specified, along with a withdrawal rate as earnings rise. For a Negative Income Tax, the threshold is specified along with tax rates above and below the threshold. Administrative considerations would be the same as for Tax Credits.

A Participation Income

A Participation Income would require social participation as a condition for receiving the income. Some people, such as the retired, and those who were sick or disabled, would be granted the Participation Income automatically. Anyone employed, self-employed, studying on approved courses, caring for children or for others who need care, or undertaking approved voluntary activity, would be regarded as 'participating' in society. Every member of the population would need to have their 'participation' regularly evaluated.

Additional possibilities

Philip Wogaman, in his list of 'guaranteed annual incomes', includes a guaranteed opportunity to earn income, a guaranteed supply of food, and a variety of other options, alongside a Citizen's Basic Income (called a 'social dividend') and a Negative Income Tax. [2] While all of these would guarantee some kind of income, only the Negative Income Tax and the Citizen's Basic Income would have the useful effects that a Citizen's Basic Income would have, and only a Citizen's Basic Income would be simple to administer.

Comparing the systems

To reiterate: a Citizen's Basic Income is an unconditional, automatic and nonwithdrawable payment to each individual as a right of citizenship. If the income envisaged cannot be described in this way then it is not a Citizen's Basic Income.

Tax Credits, Negative Income Tax, Participation Income, and Citizen's Basic Income, can all deliver the same marginal deduction rates, so any one of them could give to recipients a greater ability to turn additional earned income into additional disposable income. The differences are administrative. A Citizen's Basic Income would be incredibly simple to administer. A Negative Income Tax, genuine Tax Credits, or a Participation Income, would be nightmarishly difficult.

Notes

Preface

[1] Sebastian Kim (2011) *Theology in the Public Sphere: Public theology as a catalyst for open debate* (London: SCM Press), pp. 22, 27-56; Bryan T. McGraw (2010) *Faith in Politics: Religion and liberal democracy* (Cambridge: Cambridge University Press), pp. 268-9.

[2] For a detailed discussion of citizenship see Malcolm Torry (2013) *Money for Everyone: Why we need a Citizen's Income* (Bristol: Policy Press), pp. 187–209.

[3] Child Benefit remains universal and unconditional. The 2010 Conservative Party Conference was told that it would be withdrawn from families containing at least one adult paying Income Tax at the higher rate. This was impossible to implement because the Government does not possess reliable information on which higher rate taxpayers are living with which Child Benefit recipients, and to collect that information would not have been popular with many of those on whose votes it relied for re-election. The outcome is an additional question on the tax return asking taxpayers to declare whether they live in a household in receipt of Child Benefit. If higher rate taxpayers do then they are charged additional Income Tax.

[4] Church of England: The Archbishop of Canterbury's Commission on Urban Priority Areas (1985) *Faith in the City: A Call for Action by Church and Nation* (London: Church House Publishing), p. 224. The report references a submission by the then quite new Basic Income Research Group, which became the Citizen's Income Trust.

Introduction

[1] For more detail on the history, and for references, see Malcolm Torry (2013) *Money for Everyone: Why we need a Citizen's Income* (Bristol: Policy Press), pp. 17-29.

2   William Beveridge (1942) *Social Insurance and Allied Services*, Cmd. 6404 (London: His Majesty's Stationery Office).

3   William Beveridge (1942) *Social Insurance and Allied Services*, p. 6. The situation has recently been further complicated by the localisation of Council Tax Support. Each Local Authority can now make its own regulations for the means–tested benefit that helps households on low incomes to pay their Council Tax.

4   Richard Dobbs, James Manyika and Jonathan Woetzel (2015) *No Ordinary Disruption: The four global forces breaking all the trends* (New York: Public Affairs).

5   Richard Murphy and Howard Reed (2013) *Financing the Social State: Towards a full employment economy* (London: Centre for Labour and Social Studies), pp. 25-7.

6   Guy Standing (2011) *The Precariat: The New Dangerous Class* (London: Bloomsbury)

7   Citizen's Income Trust (2015) *Citizen's Income: A brief introduction* (London: Citizen's Income Trust).

8   If Income Tax rates rose slightly, then those paying Income Tax and not on means–tested benefits would see a slight rise in withdrawal rates on additional income. Similarly, higher Income Tax and National Insurance Contribution rates would mean that high earners would see increased withdrawal rates on additional income.

9   See chapter 10 for further discussion on job guarantee schemes

10 For an example of how this would work see appendix 1.

11 Malcolm Torry (2013) *Money for Everyone: Why we need a Citizen's Income* (Bristol: Policy Press), pp. 32-42.

12 Thomas Paine (1796) 'Agrarian Justice', pp. 4-7 in John Cunliffe and Guido Erreygers (eds.) (2004) *The Origins of Universal Grants: An anthology of historical writings on basic capital and Basic Income* (Basingstoke: Palgrave Macmillan).

13 Malcolm Torry (1988) *Basic Income for All: A Christian social policy* (Nottingham: Grove Books), pp. 6-7.

14 For instance: Philip Goodrich (2007) *Theology of Money* (London: SCM Press); Peter Selby (1997) *Grace and Mortgage: The language of faith and the debt of the world* (London: Darton, Longman and Todd); Peter Selby (2014) *An Idol Unmasked: A faith perspective on money* (London: Darton, Longman and Todd); Jeremy Kidwell and Sean Doherty (eds.) *Theology and Economics: A Christian vision of the common good* (New York: Palgrave Macmillan).

[15] Ronald Preston (1991) *Religion and the Ambiguities of Capitalism* (London: SCM Press), p. 96.

[16] William Temple (1942/1976) *Christianity and Social Order* (London: Shepheard-Walwyn), pp. 58-77.

[17] Archbishop of York's Conference (1941) *The Proceedings of the Archbishop of York's Conference, Malvern, 1941: The Life of the Church and the Order of Society* (London: Longmans, Green and Co.), p. vii. For discussions of middle axioms, see Ronald Preston (1983) *Church and Society in the Late Twentieth Century* (London: SCM Press), p. 141; Ronald Preston (1987), *The Future of Christian Ethics* (London: SCM Press), pp. 106-110; Martyn Percy (2015) 'Christianity and Social Flourishing: Theology, politics, and economics', pp. 219-37 in Jeremy Kidwell and Sean Doherty (eds.) *Theology and Economics: A Christian vision of the common good* (New York: Palgrave Macmillan), pp. 226-7; Alan M. Suggate (2014) 'The Temple Tradition', pp. 28-73 in Malcolm Brown (ed.) *Anglican Social Theology* (London: Church House Publishing), pp. 46-8; John Hughes (2014) 'After Temple? The recent renewal of Anglican social thought', pp. 74-101 in Malcolm Brown (ed.) *Anglican Social Theology* (London: Church House Publishing), pp. 79-80.

[18] Anna Rowlands (2014) 'Fraternal Traditions: Anglican social theology and Catholic social teaching in a British context', pp. 133-74 in Malcolm Brown (ed.) *Anglican Social Thought* (London: Church House Publishing), p. 141.

[19] Matthew 10:8; 2 Corinthians 8:9-15

Chapter 1: Citizen's Basic Income would celebrate God-given abundance

[1] Genesis 1

[2] Genesis 2:9-12

[3] Psalm 65:9-13

[4] Matthew 6:26-31

[5] Matthew 7:9-11

[6] John V. Taylor (1975) *Enough is Enough* (London: SCM Press); Robert Skidelsky and Edward Skidelsky (2012) *How Much is Enough? The Love of Money, and the Case for the Good Life* (London: *Allen Lane/ Penguin Books*)

[7] Tony Walter (1985) *All You Love is Need* (London: SPCK), p. 157.

[8] Psalm 24:1

9   Thomas Paine (1796) 'Agrarian Justice', pp 4–7 in John Cunliffe
     and Guido Erreygers (eds.) (2004) *The Origins of Universal Grants:
     An anthology of historical writings on basic capital and Basic Income*
     (Basingstoke: Palgrave Macmillan).

10   William Temple (1942/1976) *Christianity and Social Order* (London:
     Shepheard–Walwyn), p. 49.

11   Charles M.A. Clark (2006) 'Wealth as Abundance and Scarcity:
     Perspectives from Catholic social thought and economic theory',
     p. 28–56 in Helen Alford, Charles M.A. Clark, S.A. Cortright, and
     Michael J. Naughton (eds.) *Rediscovering Abundance: Interdisciplinary
     essays on wealth, income, and their distribution in the Catholic social
     tradition* (Notre Dame, Indiana: Notre Dame Press), p. 52.

12   Ronald H. Preston (1979) *Religion and the Persistence of Capitalism: the
     Maurice Lectures for 1977 and other studies in Christianity and social
     change* (London: SCM Press), p. 55.

13   Philip Wogaman (1968) *Guaranteed Annual Income: The moral issues*
     (Nashville: Abingdon Press), pp. 76–7.

14   Matthew 6:25

15   While I was working in Greenwich the Greenwich churches
     worked together to establish the Greenwich Foodbank. Everyone
     recognized that this was an unfortunate necessity, that we ought
     not to have to do it, and that what we wanted to see was a society
     in which foodbanks would not be necessary.

16   John 10:10

17   John 15:9–11

18   1 Chronicles 29:14–16

Chapter 2: Citizen's Basic Income would be an act of grace

1   Note that 'himself' here could equally well be 'herself'. God is more
     than personal, but not gendered. This leaves us with a permanent
     grammatical problem.

2   Peter Groves (2012) *Grace* (Norwich: Canterbury Press), p. 3.

3   Titus 2:11

4   Tony Walter (1985) *All You Love is Need* (London: SPCK), p. 161.

5   Matthew 10:8

6   Ronald Preston (1992) 'A Christian Slant on Basic Income', *BIRG
     Bulletin*, no. 15 (London: Citizen's Income Trust), pp. 8–9, p. 8.

[7]   2 Corinthians 8:1-7; 9:1-15. Cf. Peter Selby (1997) *Grace and Mortgage: The language of faith and the debt of the world* (London: Darton, Longman and Todd), pp. 138-40.

[8]   Richard Titmuss (1970) *The Gift Relationship: From human blood to social policy* (London: Allen and Unwin)

[9]   Conversely, as Michael Sandel has pointed out, market transactions corrode the norm of giving: Michael J. Sandel (2012) *What Money Can't Buy: The moral limits of markets* (London: Penguin), p. 124.

[10] Simona Beretta (2006) 'Wealth Creation in the Global Economy: Human labor and development', pp. 129-56 in Helen Alford, Charles M.A. Clark, S.A. Cortright, and Michael J. Naughton (eds.) *Rediscovering Abundance: Interdisciplinary essays on wealth, income, and their distribution in the Catholic social tradition* (Notre Dame, Indiana: Notre Dame Press), p. 148.

[11] Philip Wogaman (1968) *Guaranteed Annual Income: The moral issues* (Nashville: Abingdon Press), p. 77.

[12] Richard Titmuss (1970) *The Gift Relationship: From human blood to social policy* (London: Allen and Unwin).

[13] Kathryn Tanner (2005) *Economy of Grace* (Minneapolis: Fortress Press), p. 63.

[14] Kathryn Tanner (2005) *Economy of Grace*, p. 89.

[15] Kathryn Tanner (2005) *Economy of Grace*, p. 62; John Atherton (2008) *Transfiguring Capitalism: An enquiry into religion and global change* (London: SCM Press), pp. 267-8.

[16] Kathryn Tanner (2005) *Economy of Grace*, p. 101.

[17] Kathryn Tanner (2005) *Economy of Grace*, p. 101

[18] Kathryn Tanner (2005) *Economy of Grace*, pp. 63, 72.

[19] Thomas Piketty (2014) *Capital in the Twenty-first Century* (Cambridge, Massachusetts: Belknap Press), p. 353.

[20] Max Weber (2001) *The Protestant Ethic and the Spirit of Capitalism* (Chicago: Dearborn)

[21] Genesis 2:1-3

[22] Exodus 20:8-11

[23] Mark 2:27

[24] Romans 11:6

[25] John 1:1, 14, 16

Chapter 3: Citizen's Basic Income would recognise our individuality

1 Mark 3:35
2 Ezekiel 18
3 Berthoud, Richard (2007) *Work-rich and Work-poor: Three decades of change* (York: Joseph Rowntree Foundation) www.jrf.org.uk/report/work-rich-and-work-poor-three-decades-change

Chapter 4: Citizen's Basic Income would recognise God's equal treatment of us

1 Matthew 21:33-46
2 Genesis 1:26-27
3 Anna Rowlands (2014) 'Fraternal Traditions: Anglican social theology and Catholic social teaching in a British context', pp. 133-74 in Malcolm Brown (ed.) *Anglican Social Thought* (London: Church House Publishing), p. 141.
4 Matthew 5:45
5 Amos 5:11
6 Amos 3:15
7 Luke 1:51-53
8 Anthony B. Atkinson (2015) *Inequality: What can be done?* (Cambridge, Massachusetts: Harvard University Press); Richard Wilkinson and Kate Pickett (2009) *The Spirit Level: Why More Equal Societies Almost Always Do Better* (London: Allen Lane). On the latter, see http://citizensincome.org/research-analysis/review-article-the-spirit-level/
9 R.H. Tawney (1931 / 1964) *Equality* (5th edition, London: George Allen and Unwin)
10 Galatians 3:28
11 James 2:1-5
12 2 Corinthians 8:13-14
13 Philemon 16
14 Simon Duffy (2014) 'If Temple Came Back Today', *Crucible*, July-September 2014, pp. 17-25.
15 R.H. Tawney (1931 / 1964) *Equality* (5th edition, London: George Allen and Unwin), p. 86.
16 Daniel Jenkins (1961) *Equality and Excellence* (London: SCM Press), p 84. For a list of practical and necessary exceptions to an absolute

equality of income see Philip Wogaman (1968) *Guaranteed Annual Income: The moral issues* (Nashville: Abingdon Press), pp. 95-9.

[17] Robert Pinker (1971) *Social Theory and Social Policy* (London: Heinemann), p. 144.

[18] Matthew 5: 43-46

Chapter 5: Citizen's Basic Income would provide for the poor

[1] Luke 4:18-19: a reference to the Jubilee year described in Leviticus 25: 8-12

[2] Luke 4:21

[3] Mark 1:15

[4] Leviticus 19:9; 23:22; Deuteronomy 24:21

[5] Ruth 2:2-23

[6] Deuteronomy 24:13

[7] Leviticus 19:15

[8] Genesis 1:26-27

[9] Psalm 8:5. Alternative translations are 'little lower than divine beings' or 'little lower than angels'.

[10] Jane Gingrich (2014) 'Structuring the Vote: Welfare institutions and value-based vote choices', pp. 93–112 in Staffan Kumlin and Isabelle Stadelmann-Steffen (eds.), *How Welfare States Shape the Democratic Public: Policy feedback, participation, voting, and attitudes* (Cheltenham: Edward Elgar), p. 109.

[11] Davala, Sarath, Renana Jhabvala, Soumya Kapoor Mehta and Guy Standing (2014) *Basic Income: A Transformative Policy for India* (London: Bloomsbury); Haarman, Claudia and Dirk Haarmann (2007) 'From Survival to Decent Employment: Basic Income Security in Namibia', *Basic Income Studies*, vol. 2, no. 1, pp. 1-7; Basic Income Grant Coalition (2009) *Making the Difference: The BIG in Namibia: Basic Income Grant Pilot Project, Assessment Report* (Namibia: Basic Income Grant Coalition, Namibia NGO Forum), www.bignam.org/Publications/BIG_Assessment_report_08b.pdf, 23/09/2011

[12] See Malcolm Torry (2013) *Money for Everyone: Why we need a Citizen's Income* (Bristol: Policy Press), pp. 161-85, for a thorough discussion of poverty.

[13] Ruth Lister (2004) *Poverty* (Cambridge: Polity Press), pp. 94-7, 145-6, 178-83.

[14] Michael G. Pollitt (2015) 'What Do Theologians need to Know about Economics?' pp. 27-45 in Jeremy Kidwell and Sean Doherty (eds.) *Theology and Economics: A Christian vision of the common good* (New York: Palgrave Macmillan), pp. 31, 33.

[15] On evangelical Christians' views on the roots of poverty, see Evangelical Alliance (2015) *Good News for the Poor?* (London: Evangelical Alliance), http://www.eauk.org/church/resources/snapshot/good-news-for-the-poor.cfm, p. 14.

[16] Malcolm Torry (2015) *Two feasible ways to implement a revenue neutral Citizen's Income scheme*, Institute for Social and Economic Research Working Paper EM6/15, Colchester: Institute for Social and Economic Research, University of Essex), www.iser.essex.ac.uk/research/publications/working-papers/euromod/em6-15

[17] Matthew 25:42-45

[18] See Appendix 1

[19] James 2:2-4

[20] James 2: 14-17, 24

Chapter 6: Citizen's Basic Income would not judge

[1] John 12:47

[2] John 8:2-10; Luke 19:1-7

[3] 1 Corinthians 8:9

[4] 1 Corinthians 8:12

[5] 1 Corinthians 8:11

[6] Mark 9:42

[7] Matthew 23:23

[8] Malcolm Torry (2016) *The Feasibility of Citizen's Income* (New York: Palgrave Macmillan), chapter 5.

[9] Martin Charlesworth and Natalie Williams (2014) *The Myth of the Undeserving Poor: A Christian response to poverty in Britain today* (Manchester: Jubilee+ / Grosvenor House)

[10] Galatians 3:28

[11] Romans 3:23

[12] Philip Wogaman (1968) *Guaranteed Annual Income: The moral issues* (Nashville: Abingdon Press), pp. 66-7.

[13] Charlesworth, Martin and Natalie Williams (2014) *The Myth of the Undeserving Poor: A Christian response to poverty in Britain today* (Manchester: Jubilee+ / Grosvenor House), p. 107

Chapter 7: Citizen's Basic Income would constantly forgive

1   Matthew 6:12
2   Deuteronomy 15:1
3   Matthew 6:14–15
4   Matthew 18:23–35
5   Mark 1:9
6   Luke 3:7–14
7   Mark 2:18–20
8   Mark 7:33–34
9   Mark 2:15–17
10 E.P. Sanders (1983) 'Jesus and the Sinners', *Journal for the Study of the New Testament*, vol. 19, pp. 5–36: Could it be that he offered them inclusion in the Kingdom *while they were still sinners* and *without* requiring repentance? (p.23) (Sanders' emphasis). Sanders clearly believes that Jesus did. Cf. E.P. Sanders (1995) *The Historical Figure of Jesus* (London: Penguin), pp. 226–37.
11 Peter Selby (1997) *Grace and Mortgage: The language of faith and the debt of the world* (London: Darton, Longman and Todd)
12 There will no doubt continue to be debate as to whether prisoners should continue to receive their Citizen's Basic Incomes; and whether UK passport holders living in other countries should receive a Citizen's Basic Income designed for legal residents of the UK is an interesting question.
13 The Government is able to deduct fines and benefits overpayments from someone's benefits. I'm hoping that it would not be permitted to make such deductions for someone's Citizen's Basic Income.

Chapter 8: Citizen's Basic Income would ensure that workers would be paid for their work

1   Deuteronomy 24:14–15
2   Luke 10:7
3   Deuteronomy 25:4
4   1 Corinthians 9:9
5   James 5:4
6   Richard Murphy and Howard Reed (2013) *Financing the Social State: Towards a full employment economy* (London: Centre for Labour and Social Studies), pp. 25–7.
7   Luke 10:7
8   Matthew 20:1–16

Chapter 9: Citizen's Basic Income would be the basis of a covenant

1   Genesis 6:18
2   Genesis 9:8-17
3   Deuteronomy 4:31
4   Romans 9:1-5; 11:28-29
5   Jeremiah 31:31
6   Luke 22:20; 1 Corinthians 11:25
7   Luke 22:18
8   Hebrews 9:15
9   I am grateful to Frank Field MP for correspondence which helped me to clarify both the difference between covenant and contract and their respective connections with different kinds of social security benefits.
10 2 Corinthians 5:18-20
11 The following discussion is taken from the editorial in the *Citizen's Income Newsletter*, issue 2 for 2016, p. 1.
12 Frank Field (1996) *Stakeholder Welfare* (London: Institute of Economic Affairs), pp. 40-43. More recently: www.frankfield.com/campaigns/national-insurance.aspx
13 Peter Selby (2014) *An Idol Unmasked: A faith perspective on money* (London: Darton, Longman and Todd), p. 124. Selby blames the centrality that our society grants to money for the privileging of the 'rewards and punishments' presupposition that people will only work if they rewarded for working and punished if they do not.
14 Deuteronomy 4:23
15 Mark 8:34; John 13:34; Matthew 28:19; 1 Corinthians 11:25
16 Ephesians 2:8-10

Chapter 10: Citizen's Basic Income would inspire us to be co-creators

1   Genesis 2:15
2   Genesis 1:12
3   Genesis 3:19
4   Exodus 35:35
5   Deuteronomy 8:17-18
6   2 Thessalonians 3:10-13
7   Acts 2:45
8   Mark 10:21

9   1 Thessalonians 4:13-18
10 Ephesians 4:28
11 Psalm 104
12 See Thomas F. Crossley and Sung-Hee Jeon (2007) 'Joint taxation and
    the labour supply of married women: Evidence from the Canadian
    tax reform of 1988', *Fiscal Studies*, vol. 28, no. 3, pp. 343-65 on a
    natural experiment in Canada. A decrease in marginal deduction
    rates among high earners caused a 10 per cent increase in part-
    time earnings among higher earners. Lower earners were not
    affected. And also see Pierre-Carl Michaeu and Arthur van Soest
    (2008) 'How did the elimination of the US earnings test above
    the normal retirement age affect labour supply expectations', *Fiscal
    Studies*, vol. 29, no. 2, pp. 197-231: in the USA, when an earnings
    rule was abolished for workers over retirement age, the probability
    of being gainfully employed after retirement increased. See also
    Organization for Economic Cooperation and Development (2005)
    Employment Outlook, 2005 (Paris: OECD), p. 127: a decrease in the
    marginal deduction rate has a significant effect on the probability
    of moving from unemployment to employment. For a thorough
    treatment of the question as to whether people would work if they
    were given a Citizen's Basic Income, see Malcolm Torry (2013)
    Money for Everyone: Why we need a Citizen's Income (Bristol: Policy
    Press), pp. 113-16, 149-60.
13 Davala, Sarath, Renana Jhabvala, Soumya Kapoor Mehta and Guy
    Standing (2014) *Basic Income: A Transformative Policy for India*
    (London: Bloomsbury); Haarman, Claudia and Dirk Haarmann
    (2007) 'From Survival to Decent Employment: Basic Income
    Security in Namibia', *Basic Income Studies*, vol. 2, no. 1, pp. 1-7;
    Basic Income Grant Coalition (2009) *Making the Difference: The
    BIG in Namibia: Basic Income Grant Pilot Project, Assessment Report*
    (Namibia: Basic Income Grant Coalition, Namibia NGO Forum),
    www.bignam.org/Publications/BIG_Assessment_report_08b.pdf,
    23/09/2011
14 Romans 12:4-6
15 www.theguardian.com/science/political-science/2014/jan/22/
    remembering-the-lucas-plan-what-can-it-tell-us-about-
    democratising-technology-today
16 Nicholas Townsend (2015) 'Transcending the Long Twentieth
    Century: Why we should and how we can move to a post-

capitalist market economy', pp. 199–218 in Jeremy Kidwell and Sean Doherty (eds.) *Theology and Economics: A Christian vision of the common good* (New York: Palgrave Macmillan)

[17] William Mitchell and Martin Watts (2005) 'A Comparison of the Economic Consequences of Basic Income and Job Guarantee Schemes', *Rutgers Journal of Law and Urban Policy*, vol. 2, no. 1, pp. 64–90; Martin Watts (2011) 'Income v Work Guarantees: A Reconsideration' (Newcastle, Australia: Newcastle University), http://hdl.handle.net/1959.13/934140.

Chapter 11: Citizen's Basic Income would understand both our original righteousness and our original corruption

[1] Romans 3:21–24

[2] Richard Titmuss (1970) *The Gift Relationship: From human blood to social policy* (London: Allen and Unwin).

[3] Michael J. Sandel (2012) *What Money Can't Buy: The moral limits of markets* (London: Penguin), pp. 122–4, 130.

[4] Wogaman, Philip (1968) *Guaranteed Annual Income: The moral issues* (Nashville: Abingdon Press), p. 56.

[5] Reinhold Niebuhr (1936) *Moral Man and Immoral Society* (London: Charles Scribners' Sons).

[6] Reinhold Niebuhr (1938) *An Interpretation of Christian Ethics* (London: Student Christian Movement), p. 96.

[7] Reinhold Niebuhr (1940) *Christianity and Power Politics* (London: Charles Scribners' Sons), p. 175.

[8] Reinhold Niebuhr (1936) *Moral Man and Immoral Society* (London: Charles Scribners' Sons), pp. 233–4.

[9] Philip Wogaman (1968) *Guaranteed Annual Income: The moral issues* (Nashville: Abingdon Press), pp. 121–4.

[0] Mark 1:15

[10] Sean Doherty (2015) 'The Kingdom of God and the Economic System: An economics of hope', pp. 143–56 in Jeremy Kidwell and Sean Doherty (eds.) *Theology and Economics: A Christian vision of the common good* (New York: Palgrave Macmillan), p. 154.

Chapter 12: Citizen's Basic Income would recognise our mutual dependency

[1] John A.T. Robinson (1952) *The Body: A study in Pauline Theology* (London: SCM Press).

2   This is very different from the Letter to the Ephesians, in which
    Christ is the head and the Church is the body, as if the head did
    not belong to the body: Ephesians 4:15-16. This difference is one
    of the reasons for thinking that Paul might not have written the
    Letter to the Ephesians.

3   Malcolm Torry (2005) *Managing God's Business: Religious and faith-based
    organizations and their management* (Aldershot: Ashgate); Malcolm
    Torry (2014) *Managing Religion: The management of Christian religious
    and faith-based organizations*: volume I, *internal relationships*; volume
    II, *external relationships* (Basingstoke: Palgrave Macmillan).

4   Galatians 6:2

5   1 Corinthians 16:1-4; 2 Corinthians 9:1-15

6   Martin Buber (1937) *I and Thou* (Edinburgh: T. and T. Clark).

7   Exodus 21:10 and 1 Corinthians 7:3 grants rights to a wife;
    Deuteronomy 22:30 and 27:20 the rights of a father; 1 Samuel
    10:25 the rights of a king; Proverbs 29:7 and 31:5-9 the rights of
    the poor; Isaiah 5:23 the rights of the innocent; 1 Corinthians 9:1
    18 the rights of an apostle; and the Lamentations of Jeremiah 3:35,
    'human rights'. Cf. Anna Rowlands (2014) 'Fraternal Traditions:
    Anglican social theology and Catholic social teaching in a British
    context', pp. 133-74 in Malcolm Brown (ed.) *Anglican Social
    Thought* (London: Church House Publishing), p. 141.

8   Deuteronomy 14:22-29. Cf. Leviticus 19:9-10: 'When you reap the
    harvest of your land, you shall not reap to the very edges of your
    field, or gather the gleanings of your harvest. You shall not strip
    your vineyard bare, or gather the fallen grapes of your vineyard;
    you shall leave them for the poor and the alien: I am the Lord your
    God.'

9   Luke 10:30-37

10 William Temple (1926) *Personal Religion and the Life of Fellowship*
    (London: Longman, Green and Co.), pp. 66-8. Temple later
    dropped 'sacrifice' from the list because he came to believe that
    nations were incapable of exercising it (Alan Suggate (2014) 'The
    Temple Tradition', pp. 28-73 in Malcolm Brown (ed.) *Anglican
    Social Thought* (London: Church House Publishing), pp. 59-62).

11 Acts 2:32, 43-47

12 Mark 6:35-44; 8:1-10

13 Acts 4:32

14 Acts 2:45

15 Mark 6:35-44; 8:1-10

16 Philip Wogaman (1968) *Guaranteed Annual Income: The moral issues* (Nashville: Abingdon Press), pp. 124-8.

17 William Temple (1926) *Personal Religion and the Life of Fellowship* (London: Longman, Green and Co.), pp. 66-8.

18 Simon Duffy (2014) 'If Temple Came Back Today', *Crucible*, July-September 2014, pp. 17-25, p. 24.

Chapter 13: Citizen's Basic Income would facilitate a more just society

1   Leviticus 19:15

2   Jeremiah 7:5-6

3   Isaiah 42:1-4

4   Matthew 12:18-21

5   Matthew 23:23

6   Luke 18:3-8

7   Mark 3:14-19

8   Luke 8:1-3

9   Mark 15:40-41

10 Luke 24:1-12

11 John 8:3-11

12 Mark 10:2-12; Matthew 19:3-9; Luke 16:18

13 Luke 10:38-42

14 The Washington-based Commonwealth Fund ranked the UK's NHS as the second cheapest and the most efficient of the eleven OECD health care systems that it studied (the United States' own system came last): www.commonwealthfund.org/publications/fund-reports/2014/jun/mirror-mirror

15 John Hills (2014) *Good Times, Bad Times: The welfare myth of them and us* (Bristol: Policy Press).

16 Leviticus 24:20

17 Matthew 5:38-42

18 John Rawls (1971) *A Theory of Justice* (Massachusetts: Belknap Press of Harvard University Press), p. 19.

19 Richard Murphy and Howard Reed (2013) *Financing the Social State: Towards a full employment economy* (London: Centre for Labour and Social Studies), pp. 25-7.

20 Mark 7:24-30

21 Mark 7:31 – 8:10

[22] Acts 15:1-35
[23] Marl 10:45
[24] Galatians 3:28

Chapter 14: Citizen's Basic Income would promote liberty

[1]   Samuel Brittan and Steven Webb (1990) *Beyond the Welfare State: An examination of Basic Incomes in a market economy* (Aberdeen: Aberdeen University Press), p. 4; John O'Farrell (2016) 'A no-strings basic income? If it works for the royal family, it can work for us all' *The Guardian*, 7 January 2016.
[2]   Isaiah 61:1
[3]   Luke 4:18-19, 21
[4]   Luke 18:1-10
[5]   John 13:34; 15:12, 17
[6]   Galatians 5: 1, 13-14. Cf. 1 Corinthians 8:9
[7]   Exodus 12:37-51; 21:1-6; Leviticus 25:39-42
[8]   Galatians 3:28
[9]   Romans 8:18-21
[10] Mark 1:15
[11] Further discussion of the issues discussed here will be found in Malcolm Torry (2015) *101 Reasons for a Citizen's Income: Arguments for giving everyone some money* (Bristol: Policy Press), pp. 28, 94.
[12] Romans 8:21
[13] Romans 8:18-21
[14] Luke 15

Chapter 15: Citizen's Basic Income would both relativise and enhance the family

[1]   Matthew 5:22, 28, 32, 34, 39, 44.
[2]   Mark 3:31-35
[3]   Luke 14:26
[4]   John 19:25-27
[5]   Matthew 19:13; Mark 10:13-14; Mark 9:42 – although here there is some doubt as to whether 'little ones' means 'children' or 'disciples'.
[6]   The first specific objective that William Temple lists in his *Christianity and Social Order* is 'that every child should find itself a member of a family housed with decency and dignity, so that it may grow up in a happy fellowship unspoilt by underfeeding or overcrowding, by dirty and drab surroundings or by mechanical monotony of

environment', and the third is that 'every citizen should be secure in possession of such income as will enable him to maintain a home and bring up children in such conditions as are described in [objective] 1 … .'(William Temple (1942/1976) *Christianity and Social Order* (London: Shepheard–Walwyn), pp. 96-7).

Chapter 16: Citizen's Basic Income would facilitate the duty to serve

1. John 13:34
2. Luke 6:27, 35
3. Acts 6:1-4
4. Gary A. Anderson (2013) *Charity: The place of the poor in the biblical tradition* (New Haven: Yale University Press), pp. 7-8.
5. Mark 10:45
6. Matthew 8:1-10
7. James 1:27
8. William Temple (1926) *Personal Religion and the Life of Fellowship* (London: Longman, Green and Co.), p 68.

Chapter 17: Citizen's Basic Income would be welcoming and hospitable

1. Hebrews 13:1-2
2. Micah 5:2
3. Matthew 2:13-23
4. Matthew 9:9-13; Mark 14:3-8; Luke 7:36-50; 10:38-43; 19:3-10
5. Luke 10:30-37
6. Matthew 19:13-15
7. Mark 9:42. There is some doubt as to whether Jesus is referring to children here. The 'little ones' might be his own followers. C.E.B. Cranfield (1959) *The Gospel According to St Mark* (Cambridge: Cambridge University Press), p. 313.
8. Acts 16:33

Chapter 18: Paying for Citizen's Basic Income

1. Leviticus 25:3-4, 20-22
2. Matthew 23:23-24
3. Mark 12:41-44
4. D.E. Nineham (1968) *The Gospel of St Mark* (2nd edition) (London: Adam and Charles Black), pp. 334-5; C.E.B. Cranfield (1959) *The*

Gospel According to St Mark (Cambridge: Cambridge University Press),pp. 385-7.

5   Ched Myers (1988) *Binding the Strong Man: A political reading of Mark's Story of Jesus* (Maryknoll, New York: Orbis Books), pp. 321-2.

6   Matthew 20:20-21

7   Matthew 17:24-27

8   Matthew 9:9-13

9   Luke 19:1-10

10 Matthew 13:24-30

11 Matthew 20:21

12 Matthew 6:24

13 Mark 10:21-22

14 Acts 2:45; 1 Corinthians 16:1-4; 2 Corinthians 9:1-15

15 Romans 13:1, 6-7

16 Genesis 2:15

17 1 Corinthians 6:19-20

18 Ephesians 5:18

19 Genesis 2:15

20 Leviticus 25:1, 23

21 Leviticus 25:8-55

22 Thomas Paine (1796) 'Agrarian Justice', pp. 4-7 in John Cunliffe and Guido Erreygers (eds.) (2004) *The Origins of Universal Grants: An anthology of historical writings on basic capital and Basic Income* (Basingstoke: Palgrave Macmillan).

2   1 Chronicles 29:14-16

Chapter 19: Citizen's Basic Income would be an act of love

1   John 13:34-35

2   1 Corinthians 13:4-7

3   Stanley Booth-Clibborn (1991) *Taxes: Burden or Blessing?* (London: Arthur James), pp. 128-9.

Appendix 1: Two feasible Citizen's Basic Income schemes for the UK

1   Malcolm Torry (2015) *Two feasible ways to implement a revenue neutral Citizen's Income scheme*, Institute for Social and Economic Research EUROMOD Working Paper EM6/15 (Colchester: Institute for Social and Economic Research, University of Essex), www.iser. essex.ac.uk/research/publications/working-papers/euromod/

em6-15; Malcolm Torry (2016) 'The net income effects of two Citizen's Income schemes for an individual earning the National Minimum Wage', *Citizen's Income Newsletter*, issue 1 for 2016 (London: Citizen's Income Trust), pp. 6-9, www.citizensincome. org/resources/Newsletter20161.htm. A full length study of the feasibility of Citizen's Basic Income will be published by Palgrave Macmillan in 2016 under the title *The Feasibility of Citizen's Income*.

2 A full discussion of these results can be found in a Euromod working paper, *Two feasible ways to implement a revenue neutral Citizen's Income scheme*, Institute for Social and Economic Research Working Paper EM6/15, Colchester: Institute for Social and Economic Research, University of Essex, April 2015, www.iser.essex.ac.uk/research/publications/working-papers/euromod/em6-15

Appendix 2: Alternative options for the reform of the UK's tax and benefits system

1 A full discussion of these alternative schemes can be found in Malcolm Torry (2016) *The Feasibility of Citizen's Income* (New York: Palgrave Macmillan), chapter 6. See also Malcolm Torry (2013) *Money for Everyone: Why we need a Citizen's Income* (Bristol: Policy Press), pp. 255-64.

2 Philip Wogaman (1968) *Guaranteed Annual Income: The moral issues* (Nashville: Abingdon Press), pp. 19-37.

Bibliography

Anderson, Gary A. (2013) *Charity: The place of the poor in the biblical tradition* (New Haven: Yale University Press)

Archbishop of York's Conference (1941) *The Proceedings of the Archbishop of York's Conference, Malvern, 1941: The Life of the Church and the Order of Society*, (London: Longmans, Green and Co.)

Atherton, John (2008) *Transfiguring Capitalism: An enquiry into religion and global change* (London: SCM Press)

Atkinson, Anthony B. (2015) *Inequality: What can be done?* (Cambridge, Massachusetts: Harvard University Press)

Basic Income Grant Coalition (2009) *Making the Difference: The BIG in Namibia: Basic Income Grant Pilot Project, Assessment Report* (Namibia: Basic Income Grant Coalition, Namibia NGO Forum), www.bignam.org/Publications/BIG_Assessment_report_08b.pdf, 23/09/2011

Beretta, Simona (2006) 'Wealth Creation in the Global Economy: Human labor and development', pp. 129–56 in Helen Alford, Charles M.A. Clark, S.A. Cortright, and Michael J. Naughton (eds.) *Rediscovering Abundance: Interdisciplinary essays on wealth, income, and their distribution in the Catholic social tradition* (Notre Dame, Indiana: Notre Dame Press)

Berthoud, Richard (2007) *Work-rich and Work-poor: Three decades of change* (York: Joseph Rowntree Foundation) www.jrf.org.uk/report/work-rich-and-work-poor-three-decades-change

Beveridge, William (1942) *Social Insurance and Allied Services*, Cmd. 6404 (London: His Majesty's Stationery Office)

Booth-Clibborn, Stanley (1991) *Taxes: Burden or Blessing?* (London: Arthur James)

Brittan, Samuel and Steven Webb (1990) *Beyond the Welfare State: An examination of Basic Incomes in a market economy* (Aberdeen: Aberdeen University Press)

Buber, Martin (1937) *I and Thou* (Edinburgh: T. and T. Clark)

Charlesworth, Martin and Natalie Williams (2014) *The Myth of the Undeserving Poor: A Christian response to poverty in Britain today* (Manchester: Jubilee+ / Grosvenor House)

Church of England: The Archbishop of Canterbury's Commission on Urban Priority Areas (1985) *Faith in the City: A Call for Action by Church and Nation* (London: Church House Publishing)

Citizen's Income Trust (2015) *Citizen's Income: A brief introduction* (London: Citizen's Income Trust) www.citizensincome.org/filelibrary/Booklet2015.pdf

Clark, Charles M.A. (2006) 'Wealth as Abundance and Scarcity: Perspectives from Catholic social thought and economic theory', p. 28–56 in Helen Alford, Charles M.A. Clark, S.A. Cortright, and Michael J. Naughton (eds.) *Rediscovering Abundance: Interdisciplinary essays on wealth, income, and their distribution in the Catholic social tradition* (Notre Dame, Indiana: Notre Dame Press)

Cranfield, C.E.B. (1959) *The Gospel According to St Mark* (Cambridge: Cambridge University Press)

Crossley, Thomas F. and Sung-Hee Jeon (2007) 'Joint taxation and the labour supply of married women: Evidence from the Canadian tax reform of 1988', *Fiscal Studies*, vol. 28, no..3, pp. 343–65

Davala, Sarath, Renana Jhabvala, Soumya Kapoor Mehta and Guy Standing (2014) *Basic Income: A Transformative Policy for India* (London: Bloomsbury)

Dobbs, Richard, James Manyika and Jonathan Woetzel (2015) *No Ordinary Disruption: The four global forces breaking all the trends* (New York: Public Affairs).

Doherty, Sean (2015) 'The Kingdom of God and the Economic System: An economics of hope', pp. 143–56 in Jeremy Kidwell and Sean Doherty (eds.) *Theology and Economics: A Christian vision of the common good* (New York: Palgrave Macmillan)

Duffy, Simon (2014) 'If Temple Came Back Today', *Crucible*, July–September 2014, pp. 17–25

Evangelical Alliance (2015) *Good News for the Poor?* (London: Evangelical Alliance), http://www.eauk.org/church/resources/snapshot/good-news-for-the-poor.cfm

Field, Frank (1996) *Stakeholder Welfare* (London: Institute of Economic Affairs)

Gingrich, Jane (2014) 'Structuring the Vote: Welfare institutions and value-based vote choices', pp. 93–112 in Staffan Kumlin and Isabelle Stadelmann-Steffen (eds.), *How Welfare States Shape the Democratic Public: Policy feedback, participation, voting, and attitudes* (Cheltenham: Edward Elgar)

Goodrich, Philip (2007) *Theology of Money* (London: SCM Press)

Groves, Peter (2012) *Grace* (Norwich: Canterbury Press)

Haarman, Claudia and Dirk Haarmann (2007) 'From Survival to Decent Employment: Basic Income Security in Namibia', *Basic Income Studies*, vol. 2, no. 1, pp. 1–7

Hills, John (2014) *Good Times, Bad Times: The welfare myth of them and us* (Bristol: Policy Press)

Hughes, John (2014) 'After Temple? The recent renewal of Anglican social thought', pp. 74–101 in Malcolm Brown (ed.) *Anglican Social Theology* (London: Church House Publishing)

Jenkins, Daniel (1961) *Equality and Excellence* (London: SCM Press)

Kidwell, Jeremy and Sean Doherty (eds.) *Theology and Economics: A Christian vision of the common good* (New York: Palgrave Macmillan)

Kim, Sebastian (2011) *Theology in the Public Sphere: Public theology as a catalyst for open debate* (London: SCM Press)

Lister, Ruth (2004) *Poverty* (Cambridge: Polity Press)

McGraw, Bryan T. (2010) *Faith in Politics: Religion and liberal democracy* (Cambridge: Cambridge University Press)

Michaeu, Pierre-Carl and Arthur van Soest (2008) 'How did the elimination of the US earnings test above the normal retirement age affect labour supply expectations', *Fiscal Studies*, vol. 29, no. 2, pp. 197–231

Mitchell, William and Martin Watts (2005) 'A Comparison of the Economic Consequences of Basic Income and Job Guarantee Schemes', *Rutgers Journal of Law and Urban Policy*, vol. 2, no. 1, pp. 64–90

Murphy, Richard and Howard Reed (2013) *Financing the Social State: Towards a full employment economy* (London: Centre for Labour and Social Studies)

Myers, Ched (1988) *Binding the Strong Man: A political reading of Mark's Story of Jesus* (Maryknoll, New York: Orbis Books)

Niebuhr, Reinhold (1936) *Moral Man and Immoral Society* (London: Charles Scribners' Sons)

Niebuhr, Reinhold (1938) *An Interpretation of Christian Ethics* (London: Student Christian Movement)

Niebuhr, Reinhold (1940) *Christianity and Power Politics* (London: Charles Scribners' Sons)

Nineham, D.E. (1968) *The Gospel of St Mark* (2nd edition) (London: Adam and Charles Black)

O'Farrell, John (2016) 'A no-strings basic income? If it works for the royal family, it can work for us all' *The Guardian*, 7 January 2016

Organization for Economic Cooperation and Development (2005) *Employment Outlook, 2005* (Paris: OECD)

Paine, Thomas (1796) 'Agrarian Justice', pp. 4–7 in John Cunliffe and Guido Erreygers (eds.) (2004) *The Origins of Universal Grants: An anthology of historical writings on basic capital and Basic Income* (Basingstoke: Palgrave Macmillan)

Percy, Martyn (2015) 'Christianity and Social Flourishing: Theology, politics, and economics', pp. 219–37 in Jeremy Kidwell and Sean Doherty (eds.) *Theology and Economics: A Christian vision of the common good* (New York: Palgrave Macmillan)

Piketty, Thomas (2014) *Capital in the Twenty-first Century* (Cambridge, Massachusetts: Belknap Press)

Pinker, Robert (1971) *Social Theory and Social Policy* (London: Heinemann)

Pollitt, Michael G. (2015) 'What Do Theologians need to Know about Economics?' pp. 27–45 in Jeremy Kidwell and Sean Doherty (eds.) *Theology and Economics: A Christian vision of the common good* (New York: Palgrave Macmillan)

Preston, Ronald H. (1979) *Religion and the Persistence of Capitalism: the Maurice Lectures for 1977 and other studies in Christianity and social change* (London: SCM Press)

Preston, Ronald (1983) *Church and Society in the Late Twentieth Century* (London: SCM Press)

Preston, Ronald (1987), *The Future of Christian Ethics* (London: SCM Press)

Preston, Ronald (1991) *Religion and the Ambiguities of Capitalism* (London: SCM Press)

Preston, Ronald (1992) 'A Christian Slant on Basic Income', *BIRG Bulletin*, no. 15 (London: Citizen's Income Trust), pp. 8–9

Rawls, John (1971) *A Theory of Justice* (Mass.: Belknap Press of Harvard University Press)

Robinson, John A.T. (1952) *The Body: A study in Pauline Theology* (London: SCM Press)

Rowlands, Anna (2014) 'Fraternal Traditions: Anglican social theology and Catholic social teaching in a British context', pp. 133–74 in Malcolm Brown (ed.) *Anglican Social Thought* (London: Church House Publishing)

Sandel, Michael J. (2012) *What Money Can't Buy: The moral limits of markets* (London: Penguin)

Sanders, E.P. (1983) 'Jesus and the Sinners', *Journal for the Study of the New Testament*, vol. 19, pp. 5–36

Sanders, E.P. (1995) *The Historical Figure of Jesus* (London: Penguin)

Selby, Peter (1997) *Grace and Mortgage: The language of faith and the debt of the world* (London: Darton, Longman and Todd)

Selby, Peter (2014) *An Idol Unmasked: A faith perspective on money* (London: Darton, Longman and Todd)

Standing, Guy (2011) *The Precariat: The New Dangerous Class* (London: Bloomsbury)

Suggate, Alan M. (2014) 'The Temple Tradition', pp. 28–73 in Malcolm Brown (ed.) *Anglican Social Theology* (London: Church House Publishing)

Tanner, Kathryn (2005) *Economy of Grace* (Minneapolis: Fortress Press)

Tawney, R.H.(1931 / 1964) *Equality* (5th edition, London: George Allen and Unwin)

Taylor, John V. (1975) *Enough is Enough* (London: SCM Press)

Temple, William (1926) *Personal Religion and the Life of Fellowship* (London: Longman, Green and Co.)

Temple, William (1942/1976) *Christianity and Social Order* (London: Shepheard-Walwyn)

Titmuss, Richard (1970) *The Gift Relationship: From human blood to social policy* (London: Allen and Unwin)

Torry, Malcolm (1988) *Basic Income for All: A Christian social policy* (Nottingham: Grove Books)

Torry, Malcolm (2005) *Managing God's Business: Religious and faith-based organizations and their management* (Aldershot: Ashgate)

Torry, Malcolm (2013) *Money for Everyone: Why we need a Citizen's Income* (Bristol: Policy Press)

Torry, Malcolm (2014) *Managing Religion: The management of Christian religious and faith-based organizations*: volume I, *internal relationships*; volume II, *external relationships* (Basingstoke: Palgrave Macmillan)

Torry, Malcolm (2015) *Two feasible ways to implement a revenue neutral Citizen's Income scheme*, Institute for Social and Economic Research EUROMOD Working Paper EM6/15 (Colchester: Institute for Social and Economic Research, University of Essex), www.iser.essex.ac.uk/research/publications/working-papers/euromod/em6-15,and subsequently as an article in the *Citizen's Income Newsletter*, issue 3 for 2015 (London: Citizen's Income Trust) pp. 5–11, www.citizensincome.org/resources/Newsletter20153.htm

Torry, Malcolm (2015) *101 Reasons for a Citizen's Income: Arguments for giving everyone some money* (Bristol: Policy Press)

Torry, Malcolm (2016) 'The net income effects of two Citizen's Income schemes for an individual earning the National Minimum Wage', *Citizen's Income Newsletter*, issue 1 for 2016 (London: Citizen's Income Trust), pp. 6–9

Torry, Malcolm (2016) *The Feasibility of Citizen's Income* (New York: Palgrave Macmillan)

Townsend, Nicholas (2015) 'Transcending the Long Twentieth Century: Why we should and how we can move to a post-capitalist market economy', pp. 199–218 in Jeremy Kidwell and Sean Doherty (eds.) *Theology and Economics: A Christian vision of the common good* (New York: Palgrave Macmillan)

Walter, Tony (1985) *All You Love is Need* (London: SPCK)

Watts, Martin (2011) 'Income v Work Guarantees: A Reconsideration' (Newcastle, Australia: Newcastle University), http://hdl.handle.net/1959.13/934140

Weber, Max (2001) *The Protestant Ethic and the Spirit of Capitalism* (Chicago: Dearborn) (first published in German in 1904)

Richard Wilkinson and Kate Pickett (2009) *The Spirit Level: Why More Equal Societies Almost Always Do Better* (London: Allen Lane)

Wogaman, Philip (1968) *Guaranteed Annual Income: The moral issues* (Nashville: Abingdon Press)